Marketi

Beermat

Chris West

rh

BUSINESS
BOOKS

To Rayna

First published in Great Britain in 2008 by
Random House Business Books
Random House, 20 Vauxhall Bridge Road,
London SW1V 2SA

www.rbooks.co.uk

Addresses for companies within The Random House Group Limited can be found at:
www.randomhouse.co.uk/offices.htm

The Random House Group Limited Reg. No. 954009

A CIP catalogue record for this book
is available from the British Library

ISBN 9781905211043

The Random House Group Limited supports The Forest Stewardship
Council (FSC), the leading international forest certification organisation.
All our titles that are printed on Greenpeace approved FSC certified paper
carry the FSC logo. Our paper procurement policy can be found at
www.rbooks.co.uk/environment

Typeset by SX Composing DTP, Rayleigh, Essex
Printed in

Contents

Author's Note

Having spent the last two *Beermat* guides extracting knowledge from experts, it's great to turn to my own skill, marketing, for this one. However, it's not that simple: this book would still not have been possible without the assistance and contribution of a number of people whose expertise is matched only by their kindness and patience in sharing it with me.

Four individuals in particular leap to mind: Graham Michelli, Mike Southon, Louise Third and Peter Bennett. Graham was both my original marketing mentor many years ago, and read and commented on several drafts of this book. Mike set the whole 'Beermat' thing rolling, and has provided insights into many aspects of marketing (despite his insistence that he's purely a salesman!). Louise's knowledge of PR has been invaluable, as has Peter's knowledge of internet marketing. Over and above their specific inputs, all four have a great feel for what it takes to run a small business effectively, energetically and entrepreneurially, and I hope this has also found its way into the pages that follow.

Who else? Simon Graham is another real 'Beermat' entrepreneur who has been a great source of information and help. And then there are Ed Bussey, Nathan Hill, Stephen King, Clare Lindstrand, Garry Mumford, Richard

Osborne, Nick Saalfeld, Matthew Sweetapple and Tony Wilson, all of whom have taken time to discuss their specific areas of experience and expertise with me.

I thank all these people. Of course, any errors and omissions in this book are down to me, not to them.

Chris West
Meldreth, 2008

Chapter One: What Is Marketing, Anyway?

I ask this question because I meet many entrepreneurs and small business owners who say that they 'never do marketing'. After we've talked a bit more, they realise that they do, in fact, do marketing, and actually do it rather well. After we've talked even longer, they understand the need to do more marketing, but to carry it out in a more rounded and deliberate way.

So why the confusion? Possibly because of two powerful myths about the subject.

Myth 1: 'Marketing is something that only big businesses do.'

The first marketing textbook I ever owned had on its cover a supermarket trolley full of mass-market consumer items. Breakfast cereals, toothpaste, tins of beans: every item was made by large companies.

Nowadays the basket might include more entrepreneurial products like Innocent Smoothies or New Covent Garden Soup, but it's still the case that most big brands are owned by big companies who are masters of mass marketing. This is an activity that demands specialist know-how, marketing departments full of people on large salaries and, most unapproachable of all to the start-up or small business, a huge budget. Unilever, for example, spent £10 million on a relaunch of one product last year – Pot Noodle. (In charge of this launch was a lady with the title of Pot Noodle Business Manager.) That's what marketing is, isn't it?

Yes. But start-ups and small businesses can do marketing too. Simply and smartly, using the big corporates' techniques *adapted for the small business* – and, even more exciting, using some techniques the giants can't use because they are too big. That's what this book is about.

Myth 2: 'It's a con, really, isn't it...?'

I often hear the words 'It's another marketing trick'. We say it when someone rings up telling us we've won a free holiday (all we need to do is attend a short presentation about overseas property...).

Marketing is often seen as 'sales plus extra deception'. Sales people might stretch the truth a bit, people think, but it takes a marketer to really construct a giant lie and fob it off onto the teeming masses out there. Why, they're almost as bad as politicians...

Yes, there are dishonest marketers around. But most marketers are honest people who care about their craft, which is bringing together two elements: customers with needs and products that meet those needs. Beermat business, in particular, is ethical business, and Beermat marketing is ethical marketing. Not a con.

There's also a third 'myth' around marketing, which is more of a part of the 'personal mythology' of many entrepreneurs:

Myth 3: 'I tried marketing but it didn't work.'

Many entrepreneurs, including me, have stories to tell about marketing initiatives that flopped. The business isn't coming in; a twinkly-eyed marketer suggests that if you spend a 'few thousand' on a posh brochure or a new, animated website, that will make 'all the difference'. You resist, but as sales refuse to take off you start wondering; finally you write out the cheque. The marketer comes and weaves their magic. You wait for the results. And wait some more. In the end, you get a handful of responses: one lot from people who are clearly mad, another from people who are frightfully interested but have no money at the moment, and a few others who do £100 of business then go somewhere else. So you never do marketing again.

While this 'marketing trauma' is understandable, it must be got over. Marketing, as you will see, is a many-faceted thing (I was going to write 'many-splendoured', but maybe that's taking it a bit too far). Just because one marketing effort didn't succeed, it does not mean that others won't, or that the whole subject is irrelevant. Turn your thinking around. Marketing works — that's why the Pot Noodle Business Manager had a £10 million budget at her disposal. So why did your particular piece of marketing not work? Because fate has ordained that you, alone in the universe, are singularly useless at marketing? (I know; it can feel like that.) Or just because you didn't get it right? Learn from the experience and move on.

The many faces of marketing

It's pretty clear what finance and sales involve, but marketing seems to have so many different aspects. It's a bit like the oft-told tale of the blind people and the elephant: one felt the trunk, another a tusk, another an ear, another the tail, another – well I won't embarrass the elephant. Marketing is... what? Designing brochures? Long meetings discussing strategy? Walking up Romford High Street dressed as a chicken to publicise your new restaurant? Graphs showing demand curves and price elasticities? Turning out on a rainy Tuesday evening to attend a networking event? Search engine optimisation?

The answer is, of course, all of them.

To make sense of this myriad-fold activity, people have divided marketing into aspects. A classic division, by John Kotler, looked at the '4Ps' – Product, Promotion, Place and Price. Under *product* come variables such as product design and range; *promotion* is about how you tell the world about your product; *place* is about how people buy and your 'route to market'; and *price* is about – well, price. This model has served many marketing professionals well for years, but I'm going to be cussed and not use it. Actually, this isn't just cussedness (or even envy: Professor Kotler's books sell in their millions) – I find my own breakdown helps me more, and I hope it will help you.

I divide marketing into three main activities: intelligence, strategy and communication.

Intelligence is about gathering and using market information. This information can usefully be subdivided into three types: general market intelligence, specific knowledge about your particular customers, and 'internal' information about the outcome and effectiveness of your marketing efforts and the financial constraints within which they have to operate.

Strategy. The S-word word can frighten the life out of entrepreneurs and small business owners. It shouldn't. Strategy is largely about the common sense application of some really quite simple tools. (This may not always be the case in the corporate world, where strategy acquires the complexity of war, but even here, the great business leaders – and the great generals – all have healthy doses of common sense.) The aim of overall business strategy is to prosper, and of *marketing* strategy to sell the right products to the right people, at the right prices, in the right ways and at the right time.

Communication is about telling the right people about the products in the most effective way. There are many potential ways of achieving this; the skill lies in choosing the right ones for your market and in then using them as effectively as possible. Many people think marketing is just marketing communication, but that is a dangerous oversimplification.

The image of a three-legged stool comes to mind. Take one leg away, and the stool collapses. Trying to do strategy without intelligence is like hitting a target by waving a pistol around. Trying to communicate without strategy is like going into a crowded room and making a series of unintelligible grunting noises. Creating a strategy but not telling anyone about it is like – well, I'm not sure what it's like, but it's pretty damn stupid.

The marketing mindset

So, marketing is a set of activities, which I have divided into three types. Marketing is also a *mindset*. Earlier on I attacked the myth that marketing is a con, and I meant it. The marketing mindset is one that puts the customer at the centre of your business activity.

I can imagine yawning breaking out at this point – doesn't *every* business say this nowadays? Well, yes, they do, but sadly many of them don't mean it.

'Your call is valuable to us, so we're going to stick you in a queue and not tell you how long you'll be waiting, keep you waiting for ages, then finally put you through to someone in a call centre reading from a script, who's poorly paid and also works for three other companies at the same time so naturally isn't very interested in you or your problem.'

All the good marketing people I know feel real anger at this kind of stuff. Real anger, because they (the marketers) have the marketing mindset. Non-marketing people might feel aggrieved, but at the same time they'll mutter something about globalisation, 'shareholder value' or having to keep costs down. But to a true marketer, a golden rule has been broken. You just don't treat customers like that. *Ever!*

At a less visceral level, the marketing mindset is about respecting customers and their decision-making. If people don't buy your products, respond to your ads or flock to your website, you are doing something wrong. You, not them. However tempting your offer may seem to you, something, somewhere has gone wrong. The truth is that given the situation they are in and the knowledge they have, customers always make rational decisions.

This may sound like a burden to bear as a seller, but actually it is liberating. Hell would be trying to do business with irrational people who just acted on what George Bush called 'the whim of a hat'. With rational consumers, your job is to get inside their minds and understand what they need, what they need to know, how they like to be told, and how they like to buy. Then you can sell to them.

A cynic could disagree and cite the phenomenon of the 'impulse buy' (we've all done it) or the disease of shopaholism, where stressed people buy, buy, buy unnecessary items to calm some inner demon that has nothing to do with a rational assessment of need. These phenomena clearly exist, but...

★ Impulse buys are usually the result of clever marketing, like putting those yummy chocolate bars next to the checkout. (OK, this is not marketing at its most ethical, but it is not a random, uncontrolled process.)

★ Shopaholism is darker and sadder – but fortunately not a problem affecting the majority of customers.

Note also that both these counter-examples come from the world of retail. Other types of business are unlikely to benefit from such irrational buying patterns. 'Hey, I just felt a bit depressed, so I thought I'd go out and order a few hours of IT consultancy…'

What the quote above does not imply is that marketing has to be grey, dull and generally aimed at Vulcans. Customers like fun, spirit, engagement, passion, colour. But they don't part with hard-earned money unless they see a reason to do so.

P.T. Barnum famously said, 'Nobody ever went broke underestimating the intelligence of the public.' This is, perhaps, the opposite of the marketing mindset. (However, I'm not sure he really meant it. Barnum loved to draw attention to himself, and if he could do so by winding people up with quotes like that, he was happy to do so. In a more reflective mood, he admitted to pulling what he called 'humbugs', but added that they were 'advertisements' to draw attention to his shows. 'I don't believe in duping the public,' he said, 'but I do believe in first attracting and then pleasing them.' He certainly knew how to do the latter.)

In addition to putting the customer at the centre of things, the marketing mindset is about being systematic. The best salespeople are empathetic and customer-driven, but tend to react in an 'ad hoc' manner, reacting to every situation differently. Marketers share the good salesperson's passion for pleasing customers, but add to it a determination to do so in a way that is structured, logical and repeatable.

The marketing journey

Marketing is also a journey. This is particularly true for start-ups, but even the new-look Pot Noodle went through this process.

Sea-turtles lay eggs on beaches, then leave them. The tiny turtles hatch out, then have to climb out of a hole, cross an expanse of sand without being trodden on, and swim out to sea without being eaten by marauding sharks. I think they then have to swim several thousand miles to special feeding grounds. When I see film of these little creatures battling through the waves, I think of business ideas. Many appear, but few make it to the end of the line.

The first stage in the idea's journey to success – the equivalent to the baby turtle's actually making it to the water's edge – is from an idea to a real *deliverable*.

★ You can make it (or, for a service, provide it).

★ It works.

★ Some people are prepared to pay for it.

This then has to coalesce into a clear product, or range of *products*. Throughout this book, I use the word 'product' in its broadest sense, to mean a clearly specified and priced bundle of benefits which can be sold repeatably and profitably.

This bundle can be an object, a service or a combination of those. (If the definition sounds a bit starchy, there's a whole chapter on products later where I will discuss the concept in greater depth.) These products are ready to be launched.

Once clarified, the products have to become the basis of a *sustainable business*, with

★ enough sales

★ making a profit

★ a real 'brand'.

Then, hopefully, a *successful business*.

Marketing activity is different at each stage. What is brilliant marketing at one point is a waste of money at another. A failure to understand this causes many a 'marketing trauma'.

Marketing and sales

I've made a distinction between marketing and sales above, but would like to say a little more on this important dividing line. Marketing is essentially the creation of the context within which sales take place.

However, the distinction can become blurred. At the extremes, we can see that a brochure is a piece of marketing material, while a man button-holing you in the pub and talking about insurance is in sales. But supposing you are giving a talk at a local business breakfast. Which is this? Arguably, deciding to give talks, selecting appropriate audiences, writing the talks etc. is marketing, and chatting to people at the actual event and arranging for them to call into the office for a brief meeting is sales. Or is it only sales when they turn up at that office and the meeting begins?

This might sound a little academic, but the distinction is important. Marketing and sales are different skills, and you need to know when to deploy which one. For the start-up or small business, this can be particularly pressing (and *de*pressing if you get it wrong), as you may well have only one person responsible for both sales and marketing. This person will almost undoubtedly be better at one of these than the other, so it helps to know where you have to reinforce them and watch out for their mistakes, and where you can give them free rein, confident that this is their area of expertise.

I have met too many start-ups with a marketer on the team but no salesperson: they have all kinds of clever plans and some neat marketing materials, but never seem to sell anything. Nobody gets out there, sits in front of customers, overcomes their scepticism and does a deal.

Start-ups driven by salespeople often fare little better: they fail to develop a direction and instead rush around in pursuit of whatever new prospect the salesperson/ entrepreneur is excited about. An endless stream of highly customised deliverables results, rather than what is needed – a clear, compact list of products which can (as our definition tells us) profitably be replicated. OK, this is better than never selling anything at all, but if no marketing skills are ever applied, the business will end up going round in circles, and the energy and commitment of the rest of the team will drain away.

So it really does matter that you draw as clear a line as you can between sales and marketing, and understand that life is different on either side of that line and that people on either side of the line must respect one another and work together.

Note that this debate is really about marketing *communication* versus sales: strategy and intelligence are clearly marketing activities (though salespeople can have a huge role in intelligence).

Marketing is...

★ **A set of mutually supporting activities**
  • Intelligence
  • Strategy
  • Communication

★ **A mindset**
  • The customer's viewpoint is the one that matters
  • The customer is rational
  • Our solution to their problem is going to be systematic and repeatable

★ **A journey...**
  • from an idea
  • to something you actually deliver
  • to the product(s)
  • to a sustainable business
  • to a successful business

★ **Not the same as sales**
  • Marketing creates the context in which sales occur

www.beermat.biz

Chapter Two: **The Cast List**

The many-faceted nature of marketing means that good marketing practice for one type of business is probably wrong for another type, so I am going to introduce a cast of model businesses whose marketing adventures I will follow through this book.

There are many ways of characterising businesses. There are hundreds of categories, sub-categories and even sub-sub-categories in the Standard Industry Classification (SIC). More helpfully, businesses can be categorised by the following criteria:

★ Do you provide products or services – or a mixture of both?

★ Do you do this for consumers (business-to-consumer or 'b2c', to use the jargon), or for small/medium businesses or large organisations (both of these are called business-to-business or 'b2b')?

★ Do your customers have to visit your premises to buy from you?

In addition, though it isn't specifically a marketing question, it is worth asking if the business is:

★ 'Lifestyle' (a one- or two-person business), or do you aspire to grow a larger business with multiple employees?

Another important distinction is:

★ Is your product (or business model) highly innovative, or reasonably comparable to what is on the market at the moment? (Many entrepreneurs think the former, but they are often less original than they think.)

To make a matrix covering all possible permutations of the above would still be far too cumbersome – instead, I shall present six model businesses, based on those most likely to be interested in the material in this book (but it's worth being aware of all the permutations possible, given the above sets of variables).

1. First on our list is a small *provider of services to other businesses* (aka a 'b2b services provider'). H and J Web Design are Harminder and Jat, who met at college and are now going into business together. Harminder is the technician, Jat the designer. They have decided to serve small- and medium-sized businesses (SMEs) rather than corporates (note how the general term 'b2b' hides an important distinction between marketing to large organisations and marketing to small companies). They hope to build the business over the next five years to a point where they are employing a number of people; as such, they have planned for a small marketing budget.

H and J is a classic Beermat enterprise. All sorts of businesses fall into this category: IT support, PR, hospitality companies, corporate event organisers, security firms, new accountancy or legal practices and so on. For all these enterprises, the story is that their business clients lack some necessary expertise and outsource it to them.

2. An individual setting themselves up as a *consultant* (of every and any kind) faces similar marketing challenges. However our consultant has no intention of 'scaling' his business. He or she wants to be their own boss, and not anyone else's boss. Such a person is often called a 'lifestyle entrepreneur', and some commentators are rather snooty about this. However, lifestyle entrepreneurs create a lot of value for their customers and for themselves.

What they lack is any marketing budget. The chapter on 'Informal Marketing' will be of particular importance to this kind of business.

Mark Tait has been managing projects in large companies for many years, and has long felt that smaller companies lack these skills and suffer as a result. Recently his employer was taken over and he was given two choices: a healthy redundancy package or relocate to London. Mark is a northerner; his family are happy where they are; he doesn't want to move – time to take the money and get entrepreneurial.

3. JEBR Technologies (modestly named after the initials of the two founders) is a very ambitious and innovative *high technology start-up*. They have a piece of radical new technology which they developed at university, and which they are now 'spinning out' into the marketplace.

The challenges for John Evans and Barry Roberts are very different from those facing the previous cast members. Their customers will be large corporations, not SMEs. The investment these customers make will be massive. Yet at the same time, JEBR's 'offer' is much less clear than the relatively obvious offers of web design or project management.

4. Elspeth Scott is a trained aromatherapist, and wants to start a practice on her own – and maybe to team up with someone else later.

There are many similar *'lifestyle' consumer service businesses*: a music teacher, a garden designer, a cleaner, a child-minder, a personal financial adviser, a personal fitness trainer… 'Man and van' *franchises* belong in this category – though they should have their marketing done for them by the franchise operator, the more they understand how marketing works the better they will be able to make use of this service. (When I hear franchisees saying, 'Oh, the franchisor takes care of all that: I just run the business,' my heart sinks – but that's another book!)

People like Elspeth may think they do not need to do marketing. They are probably entranced by Myth 1, that marketing is what corporates do. They are wrong: it could make all the difference to whether their business grows to an extent that it makes them a living or just relapses into a hobby that earns a bit of pin money.

5. Sebastian and Maggie Stewart spent a year travelling round the world. They became interested in local clothing – not just what it looked like, but how it was made and sold. They now want to open a shop selling clothes from around the world, sourced from manufacturers that they know treat their staff in an ethical way: 'Clothes with a Conscience'.

Other examples of businesses in this category, which are essentially *selling to the public from premises*, are a restaurant, a café, a takeaway, a hotel, a b&b, an art-house cinema, a music venue, a crèche, a dance studio… Many 'high street' franchises – copy bureaux, estate agencies etc. – fall into this category.

6. Seb and Maggie have also decided to sell their clothing over the *internet*. They will set up a transactional website and run it as a separate business. (The strategy of running both an actual and an online business is called 'clicks and mortar'.) The online shop opens a whole new set of challenges and opportunities and requires a totally new, and fascinating, set of skills.

I shall be referring to these businesses throughout the book. Two other types of business will also get a mention: inventors (in Appendix A) and what I call 'pure internet marketing' (in Chapter 12).

By the way, the actual people and businesses are made up, but the business types, and their marketing requirements and journeys, are not.

The cast list

★ **Business services provider**
  • Business buyers need their specialist expertise
  • Keen to expand

Example = H and J Web Design

★ **Consultant**
  • Also selling expertise to business buyers
  • Lifestyle entrepreneur

Example – Mark Tait

★ **Hi-tech company**
  • Selling to large organizations

Example – JEBR Technologies

★ **Consumer specialist services provider**
  • Lifestyle entrepreneur
  • Serving the general public

Example – Elspeth Scott, aromatherapist

★ **Premises-based business**
  • Serving the public direct

Example – 'Clothes with a Conscience'

★ **Web-based business**

Example – 'Clothes with a Conscience' online

www.beermat.biz

Chapter Three: **The Journey Begins – Your Idea and Your 'Elevator Pitch'**

Most of what is said in this chapter applies to all businesses, whatever their size. Just as all plants from a tulip to an oak tree start off as a tiny little seedling with two leaves on it, all businesses must go through similar early phases.

Getting to your idea

This isn't a book on 'how to have business ideas'. However, I need to say a bit about the different learning journeys that lead to that 'Aha!' moment when entrepreneurs have business ideas.

Some people work in a sector for years, quietly learning by doing, before they suddenly decide the time is right for them to make a move and 'do it themselves'. I have a friend who worked in the lighting industry for twenty years before starting up his own business in that sector. I call this the *patient expert* approach.

Other people learn about markets as consumers, and are

motivated to start their own business by dissatisfaction with the service or goods they are getting. For example, Mike Southon and I did some work with Alison, a motorcyclist who got fed up with being patronised by blokes in motorcycle shops and decided to set up a shop for female bikers. She is what I call a *frustrated consumer* entrepreneur. 'Why can't I get a decent X round here?' is their catch-phrase, and it has generated many successful businesses.

Both these types of entrepreneur have done informal, unintended research simply by participating in a sector as an employee or a customer. (The patient expert has done much more than the frustrated consumer, who must now go and do more research.) By contrast, *serial entrepreneurs* are forever sweeping the business landscape in search of new opportunities. They usually do a lot of research before having their business idea. They like a sector; they start researching it; after a while a gap in the market becomes apparent... Of course, some serial entrepreneurs don't operate like this at all: they take a quick look at a sector, have an 'Aha!' moment, and *then* the serious research begins.

Surprised entrepreneurs suddenly find themselves propelled into a position where doing X is possible – or, in some cases, a necessity, for example if they are made redundant. By and large they have not done much formal research up to that point.

Whether painstakingly researched or a simple hunch, as long as you have a business idea, you are on the starting grid – or, to go back our sea-turtle analogy, you have just cracked your way out of the eggshell.

Your elevator pitch

You have your idea. Time to start building around it. This (for those entrepreneurs relatively new to the fields they have chosen) means doing more research. And, for everyone, it's time to think about strategy.

Too many entrepreneurs start spending too quickly without thinking their idea through properly – in other words without doing proper strategy work. Others do the opposite, and go off and write a lengthy business plan. This may sound much wiser, and probably is a bit wiser, but it is still not ideal. It's too early for that level of detail.

What you need is a nice, clear, concise, well-thought-out *elevator pitch*. I'm sure most readers will be familiar with the term: you get into a lift (or an elevator, if you're in America); just as the doors close, Bill Gates (or whoever you want to impress) gets in and presses 7. The lift starts moving. You have those seven floors to tell this person your business idea.

The elevator pitch is not a clear, planned route-map to success. It's more a manifesto or a declaration of intent, an outline of where the destination is and why you've got a decent chance of getting there.

Lifestyle entrepreneurs may think that even this is a bit grandiose for them. They are wrong. Every business, however small, needs the discipline and direction that the elevator pitch provides. OK, maybe you shouldn't bother Bill Gates with your garden maintenance business aimed at anyone within an hour's drive of Exeter. But instead, imagine you're at a party and someone has just said: 'Oh, you're starting your own business, are you? What is it you do?' You will probably have about as long as it takes a lift to travel seven floors to tell them before you begin to bore them (unless they fancy you or think you might lend them some money). What is your reply?

Fifteen seconds, starting now. Go!

Five questions

Questions 1 and 2

When Mike Southon and I took *The Beermat Entrepreneur* show to America, we met a young serial entrepreneur who said he only asked one question of any business idea: 'Where's the pain?'

I love this question. Where are potential customers losing time, money, energy, goodwill, sleep, self-respect, their temper? I prefer it to a close rival, 'Where's the opportunity?' The pain question is sharper, and focuses attention more firmly on the customer. If you can find real customer pain – and, of course, a way of solving, or even just salving, that pain – then you have maximised your chances of success.

Let's consider how this 'magic question' bears on our model businesses.

Harminder and Jat know that small businesses need

reasonable websites. Increasingly, if you don't have a site, people won't do business with you.

Mark has more of a problem with his project management service. He believes there is pain out there, with businesses underperforming because they lack his skills. But it will be harder for him to spot them, and probably even harder to persuade them that he has what they need.

JEBR have developed a product that solves pain (it's a sensor that clearly improves manufacturing processes in a range of hi-tech industries). This puts them well ahead of many technology companies, who suffer from the 'technology curse' of being obsessed with a purely technical problem – how can we do x with y? Academically, solving this problem is a worthwhile exercise, but until pain can be found *in the marketplace* which the technology can cure, then the solution is of no commercial value. Instead it's a solution 'looking for a problem' (or, to jump ahead to a distinction I shall draw later, a set of 'features' with no 'benefit'). However, people still try and build businesses out of such 'pre-commercial' technologies, because they think 'there must be money in it somewhere' and 'if it's marketed properly, it'll sell...' The latter comment (I've heard it) shows a total misunderstanding of what marketing is all about. Luckily JEBR have not made this mistake.

For Elspeth's therapy customers, pain is clear and present. She has to convince sufferers that she has the tools and is the person to solve that pain, but more about that later.

Seb and Maggie have hit on a good 'pain' idea (in a market full of 'opportunity' sells) with Clothes with a Conscience. Many people genuinely worry about the conditions under which garments are made, and many of those would pay to feel better about their purchases.

I headed this section 'Questions 1 and 2', because the magic question 'Where's the pain?' is even more use if it is broken down into two aspects:

★ What's the pain?

★ For whom?

The 'for whom?' question is hugely important, as it sets out a *target market*. Entrepreneurs are often tempted into saying that they have a solution for everybody. This can easily end up as being a solution for nobody in particular. Where is the pain hardest? Or rather – a subtler and more useful version of this question:

★ Where, among the places where the pain is severe, can I identify and reach customers easily, and be maximally effective?

These markets are often quite small. Don't be put off by that. Small is beautiful (unless it's too small to support any business). Small is too fiddly for big companies to bother with; small means you can really get in there and become an expert. Such markets are called *niches*, a term you will hear a lot of in marketing. The metaphor comes from evolutionary biology: a niche is a small, very specific environment into which a species adapts, becoming expert at flourishing in that environment, either by developing specific physical features, like the different beaks of the Galapagos finches (that gave Darwin the idea in the first place), or specific behaviours.

The business of dividing big markets up into nice, clear sub-sections is called *segmenting*. Segmenting markets is essentially an art, not a science. There are some basic categories to help you, such as (for 'b2b' businesses):

★ size of customer

★ industry sector

★ geographical location.

However, successful marketers develop more subtle breakdowns of customers by their pains. Harminder has done a basic segmentation of his market along the lines above, and decided to aim for SMEs, in any sector, in the West Midlands. He has also taken a closer look at the market and done a different kind of segmentation exercise, *by customer pain*. He reckons that he has three types of potential customer:

★ new businesses in need of sites

★ existing but rather dopey businesses which haven't woken up to the need for a site yet

★ businesses with existing sites that have become outdated (either technologically or in terms of design).

Which the three different pains should he choose? I think he should start by trying all three. At some point he will probably get a strong 'gut feel' about which one is right for him and his business. (Or he may find that the business does best serving all three markets.)

JEBR are looking to work with large companies. In the long run, they cannot segment by geography: they will almost undoubtedly have to become a global business if they are to be market leaders with their product. However, they can start locally initially, as long as they understand that 'locally' means the UK. They can and should segment by sector. Where, among the places where the pain is severe, can they identify and reach customers easily, and be maximally effective? Right now they have prepared a hit list – aerospace, defence and automotive. As with Harminder's three markets, they should live and work with these three options for a while.

For consumer start-ups, the standard segmentation variables are slightly different. Location and social class are the classic ones. Seb and Maggie have done their basic segmentation, and reckon that their shop will be popular with more affluent people. They have chosen to set up in the nearest cathedral city to their home. However, they have also 'segmented by pain': their market is people who care about global issues.

Their website has, of course, a global market, but is also 'segmented by pain' – it will largely be visited by people interested in making ethical purchases.

Positioning is essentially the same exercise as above, done not by looking at customers but by looking at the competition. Most businesses place (or find) themselves on a continuum between the very upmarket and the cheap-and-cheerful. For example, you can get a website run up by a student for a couple of hundred quid, or you can go to a design agency with offices in London and New York and pay a fortune. H and J are wisely going for somewhere in between, the mid-market option. In other words, they have decided that their target market is people who, while keeping an eye on cost, want a certain level of quality. The student-designed one would look cheap, and probably not meet all the legal requirements of a site.

Most markets cluster round certain *price points*, where people are used to getting specific 'bundles of benefit' and paying a certain amount for them. For example, some people buy sports cars – fast, fun to drive, fantastic engineering, two seats, expensive. Others buy family cars – safe, roomy, versatile, priced at around £10K to £15K. Attempts to produce hybrids outside these clusters usually fail: a sports car that also has room for two kids, luggage and a dog? A precision-engineered family car costing as much as a Maserati?

Technology marketer Nathan Hill of Qi3 in Cambridge demonstrated the 'clustering round price points' phenomenon most elegantly to me by asking a room full of men how much they had paid for a haircut. The answers were all around £5, £15 or £40. There was very little in the middle. 'I nearly always find this,' was his comment.

Question 3

The next question in the elevator/party pitch asks, 'OK, you've established the pain and a target market (which you might narrow down later), what are you actually going to do about it?' Or, more fully:

★ What are you going to create, that people can and will buy, that will fix it?

Just to solve pain is rarely enough: your solution has to be turned into something you can sell in a way that is repeatable (and, of course, profitable) – in other words the solution has to take the form of a *product* or set of products. (More about these in Chapter 5.)

Question 4

Why should people in our target market buy this from us rather than someone else? Or, tougher (but often more realistic):

★ Why should people in our target market switch to us from their existing supplier?

The best answer to this last question is what marketers call a USP (Unique Selling Point) or differentiator. In his book *Selling the Invisible*, Harry Beckwith imagines a rather assertive customer challenging you with a question (maybe poking a finger at you as he does so): 'Give me one good reason why I should switch to you.' One good reason? You should be able to answer that question.

The ideal 'good reason' is that you, and only you, totally solve a previously intractable pain. James Dyson's bagless vacuum cleaner is a great example of this: bags in vacuum cleaners were always a nuisance, and he created (and carefully patented) a unique solution to that. But that is an extreme example. Most businesses don't bring about radical change – and that's fine. A classic formula for 'one good reason' is that you are 10% better, nicer, easier or cheaper than the competition.

Note the 'or'. You don't have to be all four and, actually, shouldn't be. When I meet people who tell me they are all four, I worry that they will spread their valuable resources of time, cash and commitment too wide – and miss the crucial 10% factor. They'll end up a *tiny* bit better, nicer, easier and cheaper than the rest, but nobody will be bothered to switch to them as there will be no single *compelling* reason to do so.

Whichever three of these four are not your USP become what some people call 'hygiene factors', a necessary condition of purchase. A 10% nicer company *also* needs to be good enough, easy enough and charge a fair price.

Better can be something of a subjective judgement! Note that companies that specialise in very small niches become better by being the leading (and possibly only) experts on the subject.

Easier means, of course, easy for the customer. Easier to buy, or easier to use once you've got it. This is the USP that supports many local businesses.

Nicer. Many businesses start off selling to friends, or at least acquaintances, of the owner, and grow by 'informal marketing' (see Chapter 8). Many small businesses, especially 'b2b' service providers, never move on from this. Their USP is effectively 'nicer' – 'You know me; you can trust me (ask around if you have any doubts)'. You'll never achieve world domination this way, but maybe that's not what you want in the first place…

However, this only suits some kinds of business. And even with b2b service companies, if they grow fast, the personal touch can slip, and with it, the 'nicer' USP. If they have no other good reason to buy, customers will soon be attracted elsewhere.

Do all you can to avoid *cheaper.* This might be counter-intuitive, but competing on price is hell – especially for the small business. 'Commodity' markets, ones where the only question asked is 'How much does it cost?', are dominated by big players, who can shift huge volumes of whatever it is they sell and take a small margin.

Yes, some entrepreneurial businesses, like the low-cost airlines or those spartan Formule 1 hotels in France, have burst onto the scene, radically undercutting the prices of the corporate establishment, but they are exceptions, not the rule. They have found some brilliant new way of taking huge slices of cost out of some part (or all parts) of the sourcing/making/delivering process. Most small businesses don't have such radical models – but they still do well, by finding other ways of showing customers that they deliver value.

The notion of getting customers to switch to you needs to be looked at in a little detail. Given a 'pain', people are usually either:

1. Solving it already, using a rival or another type of solution.

2. Solving it by their own efforts.

3. Unaware of the problem.

4. Aware of the problem but unconvinced anyone can solve it, so living with it.

Even highly innovative businesses find themselves facing one of the above 'switching issues'. The Instruction Set, Mike Southon's first company, was based round a radical new technology. Their early battles were with issue 3 – 'What is this new stuff? We don't need it, do we?'. Later, their issue was 1 – 'Yes we do need it – but we've already been contacted by your rivals about it'. Given their strong USP – the fact that they had technology experts on board – and Mike's sales skills, they were able to beat off their rivals and prosper.

Looking at our cast, our entrepreneurs face the whole range of issues between them.

Clothes with a Conscience face issue 1: people are already buying clothes. But they have a great USP to help them around this problem.

Mark Tait faces issue 2: his customers already manage their projects and think they do it pretty well, even if, in reality, they don't. This is a much harder sell. In essence, he is facing the odd situation that his customer is also his rival.

Harminder and Jat have yet to decide if their customers are:

★ sleepy ones who haven't even woken up to the need for websites (issue 3)

★ new businesses who will be being courted by their rivals (issue 1)

or

★ businesses who already have a site they think is good enough (issue 2).

JEBR face issue 4 – their customers are always on the lookout for ways of improving their manufacturing processes, but can they convince anyone that their technology will actually do this more reliably and more cost-effectively? This leads nicely on to...

Question 5

This is about credibility. Arguably, the best way to express this is:

★ Oh yeah?

The trouble is, anyone can *claim* to deliver such and such a benefit. How can the customer buy from you with confidence?

The customer will probably have two concerns. One is general – does your new solution work? (If you are delivering a traditional solution, you don't have this problem.) The second is personal – can *you* be trusted to deliver it effectively and reliably? Both issues need to be addressed.

One source of credibility we discussed in *The Beermat Entrepreneur* was the mentor. Simply mentioning that X is your mentor (or non-exec chair, if the business is ambitious) can add a lot of credibility.

The credibility question is more pressing for some of our model businesses than for others. It's not hard for Harminder and Jat to show they can create nice websites, and their personal credibility will grow as they collect reference customers.

Mark Tait has more of a problem: he can't just press a button on a computer and show a project he's carried out. Even if he has personal credibility, people may well think, 'Nice guy, but we don't need to spend money on what he provides.' He needs to get some customers quickly, turn them into reference customers (more on this later) and create case studies that tell the world exactly how, and how much, he helped them.

For JEBR, credibility is a massive issue. Their customers will be spending big money with them, and, as corporates, will be particularly 'risk averse'. These people will be worried about the technology not working as well as claimed, about JEBR running out of cash or having some self-destructive boardroom battle, about a rival technology outflanking JEBR's... The new company must do all it can to establish and maintain credibility: through friends in high places, good reference customers and sophisticated, confident branding.

'The customer's perception of risk is the biggest single problem for most technology start-ups,' says hi-tech marketer Tony Wilson. 'You must do all you can to appear, and be, a safe bet.'

Elspeth's needs are a lot simpler: a few customers who will provide testimonials or, even better, recommend her to their friends.

Seb and Maggie must prove that the clothes they sell really are made under decent conditions – and demonstrating this becomes itself an exercise in market communication. Shoppers will become interested in the factory in Nepal where those colourful jerseys come from, and be all the keener to buy. In the meantime, people will wander into the shop and be impressed by the 'look and feel': credibility via branding. Their online site must be a pleasant and memorable experience.

Keep it flexible

Your elevator pitch is not something you carve in stone on day one. You will probably find that your answers to the five questions will change once you start serving real customers. You may find that the pain you solve is different to the one you thought you were going to solve. You may find yourself adapting your techniques to fit a new, more urgent challenge. Your USP might not be as U as you thought: customers may say, 'Actually, there are several companies around who do what you claim is special about you.' If you are lucky, they will add, 'But what we really liked about you was Y, which we've never encountered before in this industry.' And so on, and so on – the opportunities for learning about the reality of your business as you go along are endless.

Imagine yourself answering the five elevator pitch questions in pencil to start with. Don't leave blanks, but don't use indelible ink, either.

I've designed a simple 'elevator/party pitch' form around the five questions and their topics – pain, target, products, USP, credibility.

Here it is, as Harminder and Jat might fill it in. (A blank copy follows for you to photocopy and use. Alternatively, please download copies from our website www.beermat.biz).

Your elevator pitch

Company:
- *H and J Web Design*

1. What's the pain?
- *'No website; no business.'*
- *Companies with websites that are tired, outdated and underperforming.*

2. Who for? (Your *target market*.)
Where, among the places where the pain is severe, can I identify and reach customers easily, and be maximally effective?

- *SMEs*
- *in any sector*
- *in the West Midlands*

3. What are you going to do about it?
(Clearly defined *products*.)
- *a 'starter' website for £500*
- *a more sophisticated website for £1,500*
- *upgrading existing sites – specific projects, priced at £500 per day*

4. What is your USP?
- *Personal recommendation*
- then – *They have met us and like and trust us*

5. Credibility (*'Oh yeah?'*)
- at the moment – *'Here's a site we did for a local charity.'*
- asap – *other demos of our work*
- also – *personal recommendation*

Your elevator pitch

Company:

1. What's the pain?

2. Who for? (Your *target market*.)

3. What are you going to do about it?
(Clearly defined *products*.)

4. What is your USP?

5. Credibility (*'Oh yeah?'*)

www.beermat.biz

Chapter Four: **Research**

Having drawn up your elevator/party pitch (in pencil, remember), it's time to do some formal research. As I've said, some entrepreneurs at this point will already have a great deal of market knowledge, others will be starting with a lot less. What I suggest below is a research programme for someone with some level of market knowledge who wants to get up to speed quickly and start building on their elevator pitch.

Essentially, research is about becoming an expert on your business. This is not the same as being an expert on what you do or make. So, for example, Harminder and Jat know how to produce good websites; now they need to become experts on the website *business*. They need to develop *market wisdom*. This is, of course, something which doesn't come overnight, and is also something which never stops developing.

Much of your wisdom will come not through research but by actually doing stuff and seeing what happens.

It's time to become a nerd. Become obsessed with your sector; hoover up information about it; read all the trade mags; talk to all the people you can. Have a one-track mind! You will undergo an odd transformation, whereby general information about the economy, demographics, or anything, really, starts being filtered by the question 'So what would this mean to my business?'

Elspeth and Mark are at a huge disadvantage here – the rest of our example businesses are run by pairs, and pairs can have (and relish) long, obsessive, geeky conversations about their markets that would bore the pants off anyone else. Often the participants assume roles – a proactive entrepreneur and a more reflective, worldly 'foil'. For the solo entrepreneur: is your husband/wife/relationship partner prepared to join in these conversations? If not – and be honest – then maybe you should reconsider 'going it alone' commercially, and look around for a business partner with whom to share the adventure and nerdery of building a business. (You may have a mentor, but this person will not have the time for the number and length of these conversations. Theirs is a subtly different role.)

One thing *not* to do is get someone else to do your research. By all means buy formal market reports on your sector (though check whether you can access them free at a specialist library), but this is only a tiny bit of your marketing intelligence-gathering. You need to be building an internal, mental model of your market, and the only way to do that is to assemble the pieces yourself (and take them all down again when you discover you've made a false assumption, then build them up again, then add a new bit…). Your business partner is hugely valuable here, as you can bounce your perceptions off him or her. 'So, in order to succeed we're going to have to relocate to Silicon Valley some time?' 'No, look at XYZ Technologies…'

What do you need to know?

'Market wisdom' is a nice general term, but we can break that down into chunks. What exactly should you be looking for?

Market size is a useful piece of information, but don't be blinded by it. As long as the answer is 'big enough', then you're OK.

The *big topics* in the market at the moment. What's new? What's changing? What's making that change happen? (In marketing-speak, these are called *'market drivers'*.) Do these changes represent threats to or opportunities for your business?

There should be plenty of information about these in the trade press, e-zines and in online discussion groups.

The 'shape' of the market. By this I mean the price points around which buyers cluster and what they expect to get for those prices. Harminder and Jat have already done this and placed themselves 'mid-market' – but the more they can learn about who buys what for how much and why, the better.

Your competition. Who else is operating in your target market? Don't scare yourself here. You will find competitors. If you really do conclude that a market is hopelessly overcrowded, then it probably is time to look elsewhere, but the main point in checking out the opposition is to learn from and about them. What are they doing wrong? What are they doing right?

'What are they doing right?' has two types of answer – the first is information about the 'hygiene factors', the necessary conditions you will have to meet in order to be taken seriously as a contender for business, and the second is – are there any special, bright ideas out there you can, er, borrow?

This seems a good place to discuss 'originality'. Some businesses set themselves up as almost direct copies of existing ones ('me too' businesses). I must admit to looking down on such enterprises, but must also admit that they can make good money. I believe you should aim higher, seeking to create a truly original business that does things your way. But as part of this process, you would be crazy not to look carefully at what the oppo are up to. If a particular thing seems exactly right for your market, then you owe it to your customers to offer them that too. Don't be a simple clone, and don't copy anything that is legally protected, but don't feel embarrassed to do what corporates call 'benchmarking' – the big boys are always looking at each other and borrowing ideas. When you get up and running, people will do it to you.

You also need to develop a feel for who is going to be really stiff competition and who has taken their eye off the ball, or is aiming at a slightly different market from you.

The best way to check out competition is (if possible) to be a customer of theirs and see what that's like.

Movers, shakers and gurus. All industries have them. You should know who they are, even if you disagree with what they say. Can you get to interview one or some of them?

You will, of course, subscribe to the trade press.

Suppliers. As part of your general research, you need to get to know about your suppliers (if you need any). Conversations with suppliers often yield pots of useful market intelligence. They are also easy to organise: they want to talk to you, as they'll be wanting your business.

Finally, of course, you need to know about your *customers*. How do they buy? Why? Where? When? Do they enjoy the experience, and, if not, what would make it nicer? What influences them? What clinches their decisions? What do they watch, read, listen to?

How do you get this information?

There are various ways of gathering intelligence.

★ formal interviews

★ desk research

★ your mentor

★ casual conversations

★ sampling the competition

★ watching people buy.

Formal interviews

Select a spectrum of people to interview.

Potential customers should make up the bulk. Business buyers tend to understand the interview process better than consumers and so make better interviewees. The public feel it's a bit of a waste of their time, and are also less likely to understand their own buying processes – so talk to them, but not formally. More sophisticated consumers may not be like this. Elspeth has a product that either turns people right off or attracts real interest, so she may well be able to find people prepared to talk about their customer experiences and expectations in some depth.

If you're planning to sell to large companies, talk to purchasing directors. These people will be fearsome once you start selling to them – they have to be; that's their job – but can be co-operative interviewees if approached with a friendly, 'I'm thinking of setting up as an X supplier and am doing my research; may I come and have a talk with you, please? No selling, I promise.'

As well as potential customers, talk to industry 'experts'. There will be many of these around, and many will be happy to talk with you. Many sectors have a trade association that will be keen to provide help and expertise. Check out your local chamber of commerce. Contact the editor of the trade magazine, or a feature writer for that magazine whose work you particularly like.

And don't forget your own potential suppliers.

If you can talk with a future competitor, great, but don't bank on it. Seb and Maggie might well be able to persuade someone from a giant retailer to talk, as they are hardly going to be direct competition and the big-retail manager might be attracted by the ethical aspect of the new business. But then again, they might not... They should certainly be able to talk to other traders in Midchester about the whole business of owning a shop in that city. Elspeth will no doubt be friends with other therapists: she should make a formal arrangement to 'talk business' with ones she particularly likes, explaining that she's going into business too. Remember that many small businesses are not deadly rivals fighting over a fixed-size market, but have a common interest in raising the profile of their industry and thus their overall market size.

Ask if the person has forty-five minutes free when you could come and talk to them. Ask if you can record the interview – a simple hand-held tape recorder is fine – and add that the talk will be totally confidential: you will only discuss it with your business partner and will not quote any of it to anyone else without permission. The interview will occur at a time and place of their choosing. Their office is the ideal location, as it inconveniences them least and also offers you a chance to look at their business. (On its own, such a peek is not hugely important, but it's one tiny new bit of information, and you might just spot a detail that is very telling or that gives you a new idea.)

If you are requesting an interview with a potential customer, make it clear from the outset that you aren't trying to sell anything.

Some readers may find asking for interviews a little daunting: if you really can't face this, you probably need someone on your team who can. But if there is nobody else on the team, you must summon up the courage and ask. Some people will say 'no'; others will accept; very few, if any, will be offended by the request. Aim for five 'yes'es to start with.

Any tips on interview techniques? Obviously dress smartly, have questions ready, arrive early. Try and establish empathy with the person – where do you have common ground? If they are uncomfortable about a subject, don't force them, though there is nothing wrong with asking someone to clarify a point you haven't understood or to go into something in greater detail. Detail is usually of huge value. It's also fine to ask if they can recommend anyone else you should be talking to.

Keep your promise not to sell. Of course, in practice this could be a pre-sales visit. If you click with the interviewee, they clearly have the potential to become a customer, maybe a customer mentor. But that's to be established later.

Remember to thank the interviewee for their time, both in person after the interview and by an email when you get back home.

Desk research

A lot of research can be done from home or in a library. Try specialist business libraries and trade associations; large chambers of commerce have libraries, too.

I've already said you should subscribe to the relevant *trade magazines*. Yes, you can get them at a business library, but you'll want to start a scrapbook, which means cutting out articles and adverts you like.

The *internet* is a marvellous source of information. It is sensible to divide the information into 'official' company information and more general material, which covers everything else: blogs, e-zines, discussion group postings, Wikipedia entries, product review websites and so on. Official company sites are clearly biased: the company will be blowing its own trumpet, loud and clear. Let them blow, and listen carefully – just don't believe the hype. More general material will probably be biased, too, but in a less predictable way. Try and establish where the author/editor is 'coming from' and interpret accordingly.

Always corroborate factual information gained from the net – be cautious with any 'information' you only see in one place.

Check the date of online material: one of the advantages of the net is that it can disseminate material quickly, but this does not mean that everything on there is up to date. Many sites have a copyright date at the bottom of the homepage; if not, search around for clues.

Even if you are not planning an online business, it is worth checking out what words are used by potential customers in your field when searching online. This might give you some ideas for products you hadn't considered. Go to www.wordtracker.com, which will enable you to do this (more about this site in Chapter 12).

Your mentor

The sooner you find such a person, the better. One of the early conversations you should have with them is about your market. The right mentor can provide huge amounts of information and, even more valuable, short-cuts to influential people. 'Go and talk to Z: mention my name…'

Casual conversations

Alongside formal interviews, you should talk to as many people in and around your business as possible. This means getting out there and 'networking'. I'll talk more about that later.

Attend trade shows and chat to people on stands or to other delegates. Some stand–holders are friendlier than others – detach from the bolshy ones as quickly as possible and concentrate on the nicer ones, at the same time remembering that they are there to sell, so you mustn't take up too much of their time and distract them from potential customers.

Keep a notebook, and jot down ideas, contacts or names that emerge from your conversations. Always have business cards on you, so you can swap them with people you talk to. Have a system for keeping them and remembering who the person was, whether you 'clicked', what role they play in your market and any other special thing you want to recall about them.

Sampling the competition

Clearly this is easier for some businesses than others. JEBR, for example, have no real competition: their enemy is scepticism among potential buyers rather than other people trying to sell the same technology. Mark can hardly go out and get some projects managed by his rivals. But our other model businesses should be doing this. Seb and Maggie need to spend time in other shops, getting ideas for layout, customer service, product range, prices, and guarantee levels. They should visit potential rival websites and even buy from selected ones. Harminder and Jat should visit as many sites as they can.

How deceitful should you be in your sampling? In most cases, you shouldn't need to be: buying a jumper doesn't involve any explanations. Elspeth is setting up in a 'niche' market where everyone knows everyone else and where integrity is valued highly, so she should be honest with her fellow therapists.

If you cannot sample your potential rivals' products directly, make sure that you talk to their customers and learn what it is like to be their customer.

Watching people buy

In some businesses, you can see people buying. What's happening? How are they being convinced? Anyone wanting to set up a business with premises should spend time walking round their target town, noticing where people shop and where they don't. They should also get a local commercial estate agent on board, who knows the local market backwards.

Developing metrics

Big marketing campaigns are based on specific metrics. Two key ones are:

★ future value of a customer

★ customer acquisition cost.

The future value of the customer is the likely amount of money that a customer will bring over the expected life of the business (or, being more realistic, over the next five years). The customer acquisition cost is just what it says, the average amount it costs to get a customer.

At the start of your business, you won't know what these figures are, but it is worth establishing estimates early on, to help you decide if specific marketing initiatives are worth pursuing. Your competitors won't tell you what their figures are, but industry experts (or suppliers to your sector) might be able to provide guidelines.

As you grow, and develop experience of your business, you should be looking to refine these estimates into precise figures.

Enough is enough

At what point can you say, 'I think I'm on top of this, now'?

There is no simple answer. There is certainly no magic point when you have learnt all you need to know: you keep learning all the time, and part of that learning is impossible until you 'get your hands dirty' and actually start selling deliverables to people. However, there is a kind of 'tipping point' in your early research. Graham Michelli says: 'You start off gathering lots of facts. After a while, these begin to "hang together", to form a coherent overall picture of what people are doing and why.'

Most successful entrepreneurs say that they reach such a point, and that doing so tells them that it is time to move to the next phase – getting some sales and creating some products.

Exchanging ideas

I've talked a lot above about idea-stage strategy and intelligence. What about the third leg of the marketing 'stool' – communication? The answer is, don't do any. Yet. There's plenty of time for that later. Right now, stay stealthy, observant, thoughtful...

However, you should be *discussing your idea informally* with people. But this is to assist your intelligence-gathering, not market communication.

I sometimes meet people who say, 'I've got this great idea, but don't want to tell anyone about it in case they steal it.' Such worries are nearly always groundless, for these reasons:

★ Success in business isn't about 'having a good idea' but about putting an idea into practice and making it work. So the idea is just the starting point.

★ Most ideas aren't as original as the person with the idea thinks.

★ By and large, entrepreneurs have better things to do than go around stealing ideas. They normally have loads of ideas of their own.

★ If the person you are talking to is not an entrepreneur, they won't even try to put the idea into practice anyway.

Clearly if you have some incredibly clever piece of technology, it doesn't pay to go round telling other technologists exactly how it works. But if it's that clever, you should be able to patent it.

No doubt, there have been cases of ideas being stolen *in toto*. But they are very rare.

In order to get people to talk, you usually have to open up yourself. And you need to talk to people about your market. So take sensible precautions about copyright and patents, decide in advance what you want to share and what you want to keep secret, then talk. You will benefit hugely from being part of a general exchange of ideas, just as countries that trade goods, like South Korea, do better than those that resolutely refuse to, like North Korea.

Basic marketing intelligence

★ **Formal interviews**
  - Customers
  - Experts
  - Suppliers
  - ? Competitors

★ **Desk research**
  - Trade press
  - Specialist libraries
  - Internet

★ **Your mentor**

★ **Casual conversations**

★ **Sampling the competition**

★ **Watching people buy**

Become a nerd!

Chapter Five: On Your Way to Real Products

You've got to the point where you think you have a feel for the market. Now it's time to move on to the next stage – learning by doing. Get a customer, and provide them with a deliverable. I use the word 'deliverable' because you don't have a properly defined product yet. Remember our definition: a product is a clearly specified and priced bundle of benefits, which can be sold repeatably and profitably.

Your early sales will be a time of steep learning about many things, but the emergence of clear product specifications will be an important part of this experience.

Clearly, some products need to 'emerge' more than others.

For those entrepreneurs not offering radical, innovative products, there will already be standard offers out there. Aromatherapy sessions last an hour; you need a certain number to be effective. Small-business websites need to have certain features and be of a certain standard. So start there. Of course have a USP on top of this, but remember that USPs are quite subtle, and can take time to sink in to the market's consciousness. As your business develops, you can move away from the standard product. I'm not saying stay standard for ever, just that for many businesses this is a sensible place to start.

For others, this is not the case. Radical, innovative JEBR are at the extreme end – they are not even sure how their product will work in practice. They have to find someone who will effectively be a 'co-developer'. One of their team has to be a good deal-maker. 'We'll give you a prototype if you let us come into your test centre and beta test it…' (Beta testing is early testing done with customers, as opposed to alpha testing, which you do on your own premises.)

Unlike our other businesses, JEBR will probably have to spend some money on market communications to get themselves to this point. They will need stands at trade shows, PR, smart brochures and so on in order to meet the right people and establish credibility. (Or maybe not. If their mentor can get their deal-maker in front of the right person, who is both an innovator and a budget-holder at the right big client, that would be the ideal route, but things don't always work ideally.)

Seb and Maggie are in the middle ground – they have a novel slant on a well-served market. Ideally, they should do some early 'deal' sales to see how much value that slant really adds. However, they can't: you can't half open a shop. They'll just have to take the plunge.

They can do a little informal market-testing, however. They can get shipments of clothes and experiment with some ways of shifting them: book a stall at a craft fair, sell them to friends, advertise in a local magazine and promise to deliver personally, offer some on eBay… They might find one of these ways of selling is so wonderful that they ditch the shop and change their business model, but more likely they will get a feel for what lines people actually like and will pay for, as opposed to those that people call 'nice' but don't actually buy. They will also learn about the aggro of actually getting goods shipped from one part of the world to another – not a marketing issue (fortunately) but something they need a firm grasp of before they start opening and promoting a shop.

What do all our entrepreneurs need from these early sales? Ideally all of the following:

★ Feedback. Your customer tells you what they loved and what they hated. You don't have to immediately change what you do or make to fit this – that way lies the hell of perpetually trying to please the last customer. But it's useful information. This evaluation should be as wide-ranging as possible, and include how it was delivered, after-sales service and so on.

★ Help with future sales. Testimonials, recommendations to others, or becoming a reference customer: 'If anyone wants to know if you're any good, ask them to phone me.' (More on these in Chapter 8.)

★ A formal case study. I'll talk more about these in the next chapter. For service and 'b2b' businesses, this is the best marketing material.

Establish your price

One aspect of a product you need to establish quickly is price. The early sales I discussed above are essentially *deals*;

your customers are kindly acting as guinea pigs – the more innovative the product, the more risk they are taking, so they should get competitive prices; again the more innovative the product, the better the deal should be. However, you want to be working towards a clearly defined *list price* – the price you tell the world about and which you charge unless offering discounts.

To talk about price intelligently, I need to make a detour and discuss three concepts: features, benefits and value.

There are an infinite number of things one can say about a product. It's red; it costs £250 plus VAT; it makes a whirring noise; the person selling it to you has a nice smile; it fits into the corner of a room; we can get one to you by Tuesday – and so on.

Features are those aspects that do not matter to the customer.

Benefits are those aspects that matter to the customer.

One way of discerning whether a fact about a product is a benefit or a feature is to imagine the customer responding 'So what?' after the assertion of that fact. Does that response sound reasonable?

★ 'It's yellow.' 'So what?' A perfectly reasonable response in most circumstances – this is just a feature; a purple one would be just as good.

★ 'It'll save you £200,000.' 'So what?' Rather an odd response – this is a real benefit.

Bear in mind, however, that the feature/benefit distinction

is always relative to a context – a billionaire oil sheikh wanting a vehicle that blends into a sandy desert might evaluate the above two 'so what?'s differently.

In essence, it's as simple as that. Yet many salespeople, or amateurs in 'sales mode', still drone on about irrelevant features, even when the customer has made it clear what benefits they want and what aspects of the product they couldn't care less about.

The notion of *value* is intimately linked to this. Benefits (to the customer) create value for that customer, which in turn is linked to the price he or she will be prepared to pay. Features don't create any value for the customer, so won't encourage them to open their wallet. Some features actually destroy value, for instance making certain gadgets too difficult for non-experts to use.

The basic rule of pricing is that *price must represent value to the customer*. The customer must experience the trans-action, use the product and be left thinking 'That was worth it', or, even better, 'Wow! That was really worth it!'

A more cynical version of this rule states that price must *appear* to represent value to the customer at the instant they are handing over their credit card: once the deal is done and they have driven the 'pre-owned' Mondeo off the forecourt, then it doesn't matter. But Beermat business is repeat business, and the cynic's formula only works once. Marketers talk about the need to 'support the price via communication of value'; in our approach to business, this can only be done over the long term if the value is actually there to communicate.

For most ordinary entrepreneurs, the obvious starting point for their pricing is what their rivals are charging for a similar pain-solution – in other words, what the market currently thinks is an offer of value. Elspeth knows that the going rate for a standard aromatherapy session in her town is £30. Harminder and Jat know that small businesses expect to pay around £1,500 for a properly branded and fully functional website. Mark Tait does not have a price for his new service to SMEs, but should know what business advisers in his area charge.

Seb and Maggie have a tougher decision. How much, for example, does a sweater cost? The answer is that it depends where you buy it. In the Oxfam shop, a couple of quid might get you something. At an exclusive London fashion outlet, you can pay hundreds of pounds. They need to decide where to place their business in this continuum – in other words, the product's positioning.

The early trial sales may be of some help – but they must remember that 'marketing creates the context in which sales take place', so the prices they get when they sit at a craft fair or in a friend's front room are not necessarily a good guide as to what people will pay in a retail outlet that is branded and managed in a professional way. (The trial sales exercise is more about spotting winning products and getting used to selling.)

What Seb and Maggie should already have done is loads of research. They should have visited hundreds of clothes shops, hoovering up ideas for branding, layout, presentation, design, bags, price stickers and everything and anything else, including what prices people pay for what items in what context. From this, they should have developed a feel for price. They may have found a 'muse', a shop or chain that they want to, and believe they can, emulate. I do mean emulate, not copy. They are not planning a 'me too' business. However many successful businesses have a kind of equivalent to an artist's muse. Their founders say things like: 'We'd love to be like XYZ. Not the same, of course, but – I don't know – there's something about the way they do things...'

JEBR have the toughest pricing call of all. At some point, they will have to sit down with their co-development customers and get an idea of what the value of their work has been – or, more usefully, what the value of their work will be once the technology is refined, active and ready to 'roll out' as a formal set of products.

Many entrepreneurs think they are in JEBR's position of having no rivals, but few actually are. I often hear comments like: 'I've got this radical new idea/product. There's nothing like it on the market.' However, if the product solves pain – and if it doesn't solve pain, it's going to be hard to sell – people are most likely already doing something to solve that pain. (In terms of the four 'switching issues' on page 32, the product is in the first or second class.) So in potential customers' eyes, there *is* something like it on the market, and what is more, something they are familiar with and which they already use. What are these potential customers spending to solve that pain now, either in the market or as part of their own self-support budget?

Even if you are in a genuinely new market, you still can't simply charge what you want. It's just that you don't yet know what you can charge – customers may not know now what they would pay for what you make or do, but they will start making their minds up very quickly when you start asking them for money. Invent a range of packages and see which one they go for. Platinum, Gold and Silver service – nobody wants bronze any more – at £10,000, £2,000 and £500 respectively. Naturally, each package should represent value for its price.

This is not the same as creating a product range – the aim of this exercise is to find out where customers 'settle', and thus where your first product can be positioned. Build a range later.

There are two more things to say about price:

Firstly, remember that pricing isn't just about numbers but payment *timing*. This is particularly important for service and technology companies. Set up your pricing so that there is a decent upfront charge, for example for setting up a system. If this is not 'what is done' in your market, then it is up to you (or your sales cornerstone) to ask each customer personally for payment upfront. This requires a little chutzpah (sales cornerstones should have that anyway), but can also be backed up by argument: as a small company, cash flow really is life or death to you. Most customers will respect this argument. As a last resort, offer a discount for cash in advance.

Secondly, price is *dynamic*. You are working towards a set

of products with list prices, but when you get there, remember that the list is not then set in stone for ever. Prices are rarely stable. I'm not talking about seasonal prices, which should be built into the standard list of businesses for whom this is relevant (for example a holiday cottage on the coast), but longer-term overall market trends. You must keep your eye on these.

Guarantees and after-sales service

These are important aspects of the product.

A *guarantee* is a signal to the marketplace that you have confidence in your product. It is a hugely valuable weapon in overcoming consumer scepticism, a particular problem for start-up businesses.

For complex hi-tech products, the guarantee comes in the form of support. Helpdesks, training programmes for users, staff embedded in client companies – whatever it takes to make the operation of the new technology painless and, more important, to convince the client that it will be painless.

For any business selling a physical product, the best guarantee is 'money back if not satisfied' on return of the item. This also works well for businesses selling information over the internet, where the cost of 'fulfilment' (i.e. delivering a product like an e-book) is virtually zero. But even a service business should think about offering a money-back guarantee.

Some entrepreneurs often worry that people will cheat guarantees – use the product, get what they want from it, then bring it back complaining that it didn't work. But very few customers do. Of course, a few genuinely disgruntled ones do return things – but you want that. It provides good information about what isn't working and why. It stops dissatisfied customers going round telling people that you're rubbish. Nicest of all, it can turn a dissatisfied customer into one of your greatest fans. 'I bought this Z off them – it kept going wrong – but they were great about it, and in the end just gave me my money back, and even gave me a free Y. I shan't be buying any more Zs, off anyone, but these guys also sell Qs, and next time I need one I'll be on the phone to them straight away…'

OK, there will be a few creeps who try and cheat your guarantee system. Don't become obsessed with stopping them – they are essentially tiny parasites on the back of a great, noble beast, and will no doubt get their just deserts in time.

What sort of guarantee should you offer? As with pricing, the best place to start is to look at your rivals and see what guarantees they are offering. You should at least match these. Then think about your USP, that extra benefit that you offer that differentiates you from these rivals. Can you back that with a guarantee too? Make the guarantee as specific as possible: a delivery service that prides itself on being faster than its rivals should guarantee arrival *by 10.00 next morning*. Of course, this has to be realistic.

Guarantees come naturally to entrepreneurs with the marketing mindset. They are implicit in the way such people think about their business – if the customer is unhappy, true marketers are desperate to remedy this.

After-sales service should be offered by anyone providing a complex product. As with guarantees, look at the competition and see what level they supply. Ideally, you want to surpass that – but don't rush in and be too cuddly; there may be reasons why the after-sales service is at the level it is. (Unless, of course, your USP is centred around after-sales service, as it often is with 'frustrated consumer' entrepreneurs.)

Mike Southon says there are three types of response to customers:

★ To happy customers

- 'Great! Anything else we can do for you?'

★ To indifferent customers (these are actually the ones most likely to switch away from you)

- Find out why they are indifferent.

- Decide if you can cost-effectively convert them to a happy customer. This can take time, money and effort: judge whether it's worth it.

★ To unhappy customers

- Make an immediate apology (even if you suspect it might not be your fault).

- Offer, personally, to take responsibility for doing something about it…

- …And follow through!

- Ask the customer what they feel would be a fair solution. If it's simple and cheap, agree and carry it out.

Of course, a minority of unhappy customers may have excessive expectations or will just be unreasonable. Find a way of quietly letting that minority go – you'll be much happier!

At home on the range

Most businesses don't just sell one product, but a product *range*. How many products should you have in your range? There's no simple answer, but the key factors are:

★ what the market wants

★ what you can deliver.

As I've said, a market will have a 'shape', with various products selling at various price points. But don't immediately set out to cover every point. Start where you want to start, then build up to a range.

A simple product range has three items in it – a 'taster', an 'old faithful' and a premium product.

The taster. This is a great way of overcoming customer resistance. If you're planning to redecorate your house, you can spend ages looking at colour charts (and marvelling at the whimsical imagination of the people who thought up the names for the colours). Having decided on 'Extravaganza' for your loo, you then go out and buy a tiny pot of the stuff to paint on your wall to see if it actually looks like the little rectangle on the chart. If you like this taster, you then go and buy the big pots and get painting.

What would make a good taster for your business? Think of the smallest version of your full product that you could sensibly sell to customers who are interested but still a little sceptical. Mark could sell a day's consultancy. H and J could do a day's 'website audit', looking at tired existing sites and suggesting ways of pepping them up.

Note that this should not be a free offer, but a chargeable product that brings benefit. Many people equate 'free' with 'valueless', so you must send out a clear message that anything you produce is of value.

The *old faithful* is the standard bundle of benefits that most of your customers seem to want. This is not be confused with the standard product 'out there'. It's *your* standard product, which, if you have a fantastic USP, might have developed a long way from the standard product. Many businesses flourish by churning these out – though entrepreneurs can get bored with old faithfuls and itch to move on to more exotic offers.

At the top of the range, have a *premium product*. There is psychology behind this: research shows that people are keener to buy ordinary price products if they have been told about a more upmarket version. They feel they are getting a bargain. So even if nobody buys it, having a premium product available is of use. In reality, some people who 'have to have the best' will go for this option. Remember, of course, that the option must offer real value, not just be the old faithful dolled up with a big price ticket on for suckers.

Elspeth could offer some kind of deluxe service. I'm not an aromatherapist so have no idea what that would involve, but she should get together with her partner, or whoever she discusses business with, and talk it through.

Harminder and Jat could offer a platinum service for web fanatics who not only want arcane bells and whistles but also want to spend hours talking to H or J about it and be allowed to keep changing their mind.

Upselling

While we are on the subject of extending outwards from the core product, it's a good time to ask a magic marketing question: 'What else do my customers want that I can provide?'

Elspeth should start thinking about offering her clients other benefits – the chance to buy the oils she uses, a course or a book on how to use them, tapes of 'new age' music, scented candles and so on.

Harminder and Jat could add a service where they maintain the sites they have built, not just passively but actively offering the client suggestions, tips and advice. Mark Tait should look to do the same – having managed a specific project for a company, what could he do to make it worth that company's while to keep him on board, paying a retainer? It's a much harder sell than for H and J, however.

Once your business is up and running, you can be endlessly entrepreneurial about this. Try an 'upsell' and see if your customers want it. If they do, build on it; if they don't, then drop it. A big mistake is to push it even harder: this will annoy customers, who have already decided this doesn't represent value to them.

The product adoption cycle

This is something that only JEBR need to understand. While our entrepreneurs would do well to be aware of it, it is essentially a model of how radically innovative products are accepted by the marketplace, and given that it is so specialised, I have put it in Appendix B.

We have come a long way in this chapter. The idea has been road-tested with a few favoured customers, and has been brought to life as a range of products, with clear benefits and prices. It is now time for the adventure to enter a new phase – of hitting the target market as a whole.

Products

★ **Clearly defined 'bundles of benefit'**
  - Work towards the exact contents of each bundle over early sales

★ **Pricing**
  - An expression of value to the customer
  - Begin by looking at the existing market
  - Remember, price is dynamic

★ **Guarantees**
  - Express your confidence…
  - …especially in your USP

★ **After-sales service**
  - Three types of response to customers

★ **Product range**
  - Taster
  - Old faithful
  - Premium product

★ **Upselling**
  - 'What else might my customers want?'

www.beermat.biz

Chapter Six: **Your Basic Communications Kit**

In this chapter, I want to look at the early stages of market communication. But first, some general observations on the subject.

Marketing communication, or 'marcomms', is a part of marketing that is often mistaken by non-marketers for the whole of 'what marketing is'. You know better than this, but the fault is common, so needs to be borne in mind when you hear people sounding off about 'marketing', especially in a negative sense. Do they mean marketing or just marcomms?

Four magic questions

There are four magic questions that need to be asked of any piece of 'marcomms'.

1. Who are you communicating with?

2. What do you want them to do as a result of receiving your communication?

3. What evidence do you have that it will work?

4. (After it has been issued) Has it actually worked?

The answer to Question 1 is 'your target market'. Some big corporate PR is aimed at other 'publics', but a small business rarely has a desperate need to do this, so shouldn't spend time or money on it. Instead, target, target, target. Use specialist magazines, or local papers, or even parish magazines. Learn what your target market reads, listens to, watches... The internet has revolutionised targeting (more on this in Chapter 12) – but for now, note the targeting power of 'pay-per-click' advertising.

As well as targeting the right media, make sure the piece speaks to the market in their language. An ad for surfers would be couched in totally different words than one for retirement homes. Your own criteria for elegance, and even 'house style', should be subservient to this.

Question 2 is a reminder that the only point of communicating with the market is to get it to do something. Again, big companies can plug away at abstract stuff like changing attitudes or building brand recognition. Small ones don't have this luxury. Of course you want to 'raise brand awareness' – but that's a valuable sideline: your communication must do other things as well.

The opposite is what Graham Michelli calls 'Coo-ee advertising'. Marketing communication is not cheap, and to splurge money just to say 'Hey, everybody, look at us!' is a waste. You should be telling potential customers how you can solve their pain, in that special way inherent in your USP, and you should be showing them how they can do this, moving them to take an action – to come to a demonstration, visit the site, cut out the coupon and redeem it at the store... Adverts should always make a clear, specific offer to the recipient.

It's easy for entrepreneurs to come up with catchy-sounding slogans and to fall in love with them. Why not, if it makes you enjoy your business more? But if all they say is 'Look at us!', then they should be kept for private consumption, as part of your vision rather than something for the public.

Having created a piece of communication in the spirit of the above, it is helpful to subject it to some kind of measure-ment. Exactly what and how much depends on the piece.

When you are starting out, it is often difficult to pre-test. Just communicate and see what happens. But you can start monitoring the effect at once. All adverts ought to have built-in tracking mechanisms in them – a special number to call or a coupon with a specific reference number on it. PR is harder to monitor – you have to use common sense. Have the phones been busier after that piece in the *Bugle*? If so, how much busier? Measuring is all about numbers, not 'feel'. Find a metric, however indirect.

A communications starter kit

Start simple. For most small businesses, this means:

★ a name

★ a domain name

★ simple stationery

★ a phone number

★ simple business cards

★ a basic website

★ ? a logo

★ a house style.

Your name

This may be the first marketing communication tool you develop. It's also one of the most important, and is worth spending time on.

Ideally, the name should tell the world about the pain you solve and/or your USP. In consumer markets, it should also be catchy and memorable.

'Clothes with a Conscience' seems to me a reasonable, but not stunning, name. It captures the USP nicely, but is a bit long-winded. I'd prefer to see it as a 'strapline', following a snappier brand name. A strapline is an explanatory line after a title. *The Beermat Entrepreneur* had the strapline *How to turn a good idea into a great business.*

What should Seb and Maggie do to find a good name? I think the answer is kick a lot of ideas about and see if any have 'the magic'. Maybe invite some friends over, explaining that the invite comes with a duty to 'brainstorm' names, crack open some wine and let the ideas flow... When they have come up with some good ones, Google them to make sure nobody else has got there first. Then decide.

There's a nice section on naming in *Anyone Can Do It*, the book about how the Hashemis founded the Coffee Republic chain of coffee bars. The bars had the provisional name of Java Express, but neither of the founders was happy with that. Then Sahar Hashemi thought of Coffee Republic, and knew at once that was right.

If Seb and Maggie can't think of a great name, then 'Clothes with a Conscience' will do. It's better to be a bit dull but get across the USP loud and clear than to be flashy and leave people saying 'so what?'

In my view, one-person businesses are much better off not having a name at all, other than that of the individual. People's names are actually quite memorable, and easy to trace, and anyway much of the USP of a one-person business is the character of the person. Mark has this idea of calling himself 'Dynamic Projects', but he'd be much better off using his own name and thinking carefully about how he presents it.

Mark Tait. Project management for SMEs is a start. (*SMEs* is maybe a bit business-schoolish. *Small/medium businesses* sounds a bit dull – how about *growing businesses*?) Later, when he starts taking on jobs where he has to get others in to help him, he could restyle himself *Mark Tait and Associates*.

Harminder is given to flights of fancy and wants to call the company 'Flying Stallion'. Jat thinks this is rubbish: 'H and J Website Design' would be fine. I'm with Jat on this one.

Similarly our hi-tech company JEBR is fine with that name.

Note that this discussion is about company names rather than product names – we haven't finalised the products yet.

A domain name

Register the obvious one as soon as possible. (As I write this, clotheswithaconscience.com has gone, but clotheswithaconscience.co.uk is still available. Get on with it, Maggie and Seb!) If your business is named after you, then you've probably missed .com or .co.uk, unless your name is Almeric Fishpaste III Jr. (in which case, all that teasing at school proved worth enduring after all: you can have a .com website!). I have to make do with chriswest.info.

You could also think again of your USP, and think of some good alternative names, then check them on wordtracker (see p.175).

Stationery

You'll need proper compliment slips and notepaper for letters and invoices. Don't spend a fortune on these yet – you may suddenly change the company name (or the idea may not take off).

When you register the company (see *Finance on a Beermat* to find out more about this), letters and invoices have to say *Registered in England and Wales at Companies House, number 123456* on the bottom (if you're English or Welsh). Invoices also need a VAT number if you are VAT registered.

Don't forget to put your web address on all your communications material.

A phone number

Can you get a nice, memorable one for the business?

Business cards

For small businesses, keep these simple to start with. JEBR
will need smart ones from the word go – all part of their
drive for credibility.

Everyone at beermat.biz has business cards with their mug-
shots on. It helps recipients remember who you are a few
days after that networking event where you met and had
such an interesting conversation. I recommend this – once
the business is up and running: there's no sense in
incurring the cost of this so early on.

Gimmicky business cards are a real pain. If they're a funny
size, you can bet they'll be thrown away very quickly,
unless the recipient has fallen in love with you. Shortly
after the dotcom era, I had a meeting with a character from
a very large consultancy firm who said he'd 'moved
beyond business cards', and scribbled his name for me with
a leaky pen on a tatty piece of paper. He was equally
irritating for the rest of the meeting, and the paper went in
the bin the moment he had gone.

The above list is a very basic one. If for some reason you

make a couple of sales then find the idea seems to run out of steam, you won't have wasted too much money.

But you want to press on. Excellent!

A *website*

Every twenty-first-century business should have a website. It doesn't have to be grand, though obviously H and J Web Design needs to have a site that impresses, not with cleverness, but with simple, attractive design and the ability to get their message across clearly and effectively.

A basic site has:

★ A 'homepage' with your five elevator pitch questions answered. Put your phone number on here, too.

★ A 'who are we?' page with a relevant biography of you and, if you have a team, your team. These should contain things that customers will find encouraging and reassuring (professional experience should dominate, not your entire life-story. But add a human touch, too). Biogs should also be accompanied by a photo. If you only have terrible photos of yourself, get proper ones done!

★ A 'contact us' page, with the phone number (again), address (physical and email) and, if appropriate, an easily downloadable map of how to get to your premises. A link to a national mapping site will do if you can't get a map, but keep checking that the link works. Ideally the map should come with clear, correct instructions: check them by driving the route.

Soon you will be adding case studies and other exciting stuff, but get the basic site up there now!

A logo?

A logo is a visual 'symbol' of the business, often, but not always, involving its name. Examples abound. The Michelin Man. The Red Cross. The Union Jack. The 'mastheads' of our national newspapers. The logo should express the 'brand values' of the business, by-passing our rational response to simple words, effectively smuggling their message into the viewer's mind. As such, creating logos is a job for professionals.

Naturally these people charge for their work, so in keeping with the Beermat approach of not spending money unless you have to, I don't insist on logos for very-early-stage businesses. Are you really sure of your brand values? Probably not. Then why spend money on a logo? Unlike a trading name, a logo is not a necessity.

However, most small business owners like the idea of having a logo. If that makes them happy, why not? (That sounds flip, but I mean it. Starting a business is hard, and sometimes people get really fed up with it. If your logo makes you more affectionate towards this thing that is in danger of taking over your life, then it's providing a useful service.)

Our small service business owners all want logos. Elspeth has decided on a flower: nice, but she must avoid clip art (naff) or one she's drawn herself (unless it's simple, bold and clear). Mark has a mate in a marketing agency who came up with the idea of a plunger – for unblocking your business. That has genuine potential to 'smuggle' valuable brand information, as long as Mark brings the right mixture of humour and gravitas to carry it off: too jokey, and he'll just look frivolous; too earnest, and it will look all wrong. Harminder still wants a flying horse: it'll do less damage as a logo than as a name, so to keep him happy, Jat has agreed.

These businesses should find a small design agency that will run them up a logo for a few hundred pounds, as well as designing some stationery and business cards.

JEBR need to have a more thorough job done. They need to 'look the part' from early on, to convince those sceptical corporate buyers that they mean business. Seb and Maggie have to get the design for their shop and site sorted, too.

A note of caution. When entrepreneurs – or big companies – go around saying 'Look at my logo!', the only rational response is something like 'Your offer must be pretty appalling if that's the best thing you can say about your business.' They are part of your marketing communication, not a substitute for it.

House style

Every business should start thinking of the overall 'Look' of their communications. Typeface, colour, amount of white space... You have to do this, so pay attention to it and get it right.

It really is best to talk to a professional graphic designer. But if you don't know any and you're on a really tight budget, then follow common sense.

★ A clear and appropriate typeface. 'Clear' is obvious: avoid fancy or unreadable typefaces at all costs. Appropriate? Different typefaces send different messages. Do you want to be seen as clinical or cuddly, traditional or modern? The website www.esperfonto.com will, in theory, choose a typeface for you.

There are two sorts of typeface, serif or non-serif. As a general rule, for on-page communication, choose a serif typeface for your 'body' (main information-conveying) text and partner it with non-serif headings. For online text, turn these around.

The esperfonto website will give you suggestions for good matches of body text and heading faces. Choose ones you like, and try them on your friends. Ask 'Which one do you like?' rather than 'Do you like this one?'

★ Use 'white space'. Don't cram your documents too full of text. If you have a lot to say, allow it to 'breathe' by using two pages rather than one. Look at the ads in newspapers – large areas of this highly expensive space is taken up by... space. Leave decent margins on any document, and space at the top and bottom of a page. Have proper spacing between lines of text.

★ Remember that readability is all. If you want to use coloured paper, make it a light pastel colour against which text will still stand out.

Case studies

These are wonderful things, which provide essential intelligence and make excellent communications material – and should also help you formulate strategy.

When a sale is completed (which means, remember, *both* money in the bank *and* a happy customer), ask the customer to 'tell the story of the purchase and the experience of the product'. Like all good stories, a case study should have a beginning, a middle and an end:

★ Beginning. Our 'pain'. What we were then doing about it, solutions we had tried and rejected. Hollywood script models end the beginning section with what they call the 'inciting incident' – in this case, hearing about you and your product.

★ Middle. How we bought the product, at what price etc. How it was put to use, including anything that went wrong, or could have been done better. Any snags encountered and overcome.

★ End. Pain gone or lessened. Where expectations were met, not met or exceeded. Were there any unexpected benefits?

★ Coda. Were there any subsequent hitches, and how were they handled?

★ Analysis. What value did the product add? Give a numerical answer: it saved us 8 man-hours, or saved us £1,000, or bought in £3,000 worth of business, or whatever metric feels most important to the client. What should be done better next time?

Clearly this model is aimed at a reasonably complex business-to-business sell, but the basic principle of talking customers through the experience of discovering, buying and using your product applies across all enterprises.

As marketing *intelligence*, case studies will help you towards understanding which aspects of the product are wanted in the marketplace and which ones are not, and what customers consider your product is worth. In other words, they will shed light on features, benefits and value. This feeds straight into your *strategy*, of course…

As marketing *communication*, case studies make great material to put on your website, or (as we'll discover later) material for PR. Clearly you have to ensure that the customer is happy to be cited, either by name, or obliquely as 'a small engineering company near Manchester'. Be as specific as the client is happy with.

Marketing communications – the basics

★ It's part of marketing, not the whole story

★ **Four magic questions**
   1. Who are you communicating with?
   2. What do you want them to do as a result of receiving your communication?
   3. What evidence do you have that it will work?
   4. (After it has been issued) Has it actually worked?

★ **A starter kit**
   • A name

   • A domain name

   • Simple stationery

   • A phone number

   • Simple business cards

   • A website

   • ? A logo

   • A house style

★ **Case studies**
   • Beginning, middle and end

www.beermat.biz

Chapter Seven: **Your Take-Off Strategy**

Before hitting the market full on, it is worth doing a bit of strategic thinking, to plan what I call your 'take-off'.

Up until now, your focus has been on customers and competition. There is a third set of players I would like to introduce, who may or may not help you build your business. These are other businesses, which can be loosely termed *strategic allies*. Or, more precisely:

★ intermediaries

★ large strategic allies

★ small strategic allies.

As usual in marketing, one size does not fit all. Some businesses will benefit from these, others won't. Mike's company The Instruction Set did not use any of the above (or rather, they did occasionally, but found that the intermediaries were always more trouble than they were worth). Other businesses use these and thrive.

Routes to market

This isn't about vans getting lost on the A1234, but about

whose hands the product passes through to get to the final customer. For example, a maker of fruit cordials could:

★ sell bottles of cordial to a supermarket chain

★ sell bottles of cordial to small local retailers

★ sell bottles of cordial to one food outlet only, via an exclusive deal

★ sell bottles of cordial direct to the public from their farm or factory

★ sell bottles of cordial over the internet from an online shop

★ sell bottles of cordial over the internet via eBay

★ sell bottles of cordial to a company which 'bundles them in' with other products, then sells the bundle to the public, for example as a picnic hamper

★ team up with some other suppliers of quality food/drink products to create and sell hampers

★ team up with some other manufacturers of quality food/drink products to create a 'food and drink club' (including visits to producers, talks on quality food, a monthly magazine etc.)

★ sell tankloads of cordial to another company to bottle and market

★ sell tankloads of cordial to supermarkets to bottle themselves as an 'own brand'.

Or, of course, a selection of these. Each one represents a different route to market. Which one is best? The answer, as often in marketing, is that it depends on all sorts of variables, which will vary from case to case. The main thing is to be aware that different routes to market exist, and to consider the options.

You will probably find certain standard routes to market prevail in your sector. New cars are sold by appointed dealers. Baked beans are sold by supermarkets. There is normally a reason for this, so unless you have strong, contrarian views on the subject, start by following the crowd. The route is already clear, and, most important of all, customers are already happy buying that way. (If, of course, you *do* have strong, contrarian views, then this can be a powerful USP. Examples abound, from the huge range of products you can only buy over the internet, to those Christmas cakes you can only order by post from America.)

Our web designers, Harminder and Jat, are planning to grow their business by the simplest route: *direct selling* — finding businesses in need of sites and providing them. They might end up following a different route, if they do some work for a large marketing communications agency who likes their work and starts using them as *subcontractors*. This would mean a lower margin but would take away some of the hassle of finding customers.

Mark may well find his attempts at direct selling flounder because of customer ignorance. Could he subcontract to an established business adviser?

Elspeth might find that subcontracting to an enlightened local GP is the best way to guarantee work. Or is there a 'complementary medicine centre' opening in her local town, where she could practise as part of a team of diverse specialists?

Inventors often think they should market their products, even if they are much better at inventing than at marketing. They should not: a much better route to market for them is to license the invention to an established business with manufacturing capacity, marketing skills and an established customer base. (More on this in Appendix A.)

Other routes to market include using *agents*, who take a commission on selling your product, and *distributors* or *resellers*, who buy the product off you, then sell it on at a profit. These types of intermediary are becoming less popular for a number of reasons:

★ 'Channel conflict' can occur when an intermediary's interest clashes with yours. For example, your agent also deals with other suppliers like yourself. If a big customer is unhappy with your product, the agent – who needs to keep the big customer happy – will find it easiest simply to stop supplying your product and switch to another of his or her suppliers.

★ Intermediaries expect a margin on your product.

★ The internet means that online vendors like Seb and Maggie can now sell worldwide without any agents.

★ Agents 'get in the way of your communication with the customer'. JEBR will need to go global, but they must also sell their highly technical product themselves. Sadly, there is no way the founders can avoid spending a lot of time on aeroplanes: in the next few years, they are going to see a lot of the world, or at least a lot of the world's airports and hotels.

The Beermat approach to business has always emphasised direct selling and direct delivery. This is the easiest and most controllable way of doing things. However, as Harminder, Jat and Mark may discover, it is not automatically the right one. There are other routes to market that need to be looked at, though they are less likely to be at the forefront of your mind when you are starting out.

Franchising is a way of replicating a successful business. Essentially you create a formula, then people pay to use that formula, in clearly defined territories so they do not clash.

Franchising works well in retail: once Seb and Maggie have not only got their shop up and running, but know exactly what it should look like, 'feel like' and how it should run, then they might consider franchising as a way of expanding.

Both Elspeth's and our web designers' businesses are too dependent on their owners' 'touch', flair and skill to be franchisable. If Mark Tait could turn his project-management skills into a set of tools for small businesses that clearly helped them get things done effectively and quickly (which is what he should be looking to do anyway), he could sell these tools and the right to use them to selected franchisees.

The franchise model is of no interest to JEBR.

Multi-level marketing (MLM) is a system where you get people to join a kind of club that entitles them to sell your products (so it is actually much more about sales than marketing, despite its name). Club members also get revenue from recruiting new members, via a cut of any money the new members produce. The US company Amway is the classic example of this.

MLM is sometimes confused with *pyramid schemes*, which are cons. These are schemes where you are asked to sign up and send some money to the person who has recruited you. Your job is then to recruit more people who will send money to you, and who then have to recruit more people to send money to them, and so on… No products change hands, just money. Naturally the thing collapses, as it requires an exponentially increasing number of people joining to keep it going, whereas in practice the number of suckers out there is limited.

In theory, the difference between MLM and pyramids is obvious: in legitimate MLM, real goods change hands and you only receive commissions on these goods. As long as the goods keep selling, there is a real business with real, happy customers getting value from the products and a rather complex (and to many people annoyingly messianic) but functioning sales system. In pyramid schemes, you get paid for recruiting people, not for selling anything, so no value is created. In practice, the line can get blurred if goods do change hands (so it looks like legal MLM) but they turn out to be sub-standard or worthless (so it is effectively a pyramid scheme).

Ponzi schemes are cons similar to pyramid schemes. Pyramid schemes admit that the way they make money is by attracting more and more investors; Ponzi schemes claim magical powers of capital appreciation. A recent one in America claimed to be able to achieve amazing returns by using biblical prophecies – and demonstrated these powers at first, though in fact what they were doing was paying back early investors with money gleaned from new ones. The entire economy of Albania, newly liberated from Stalinism, was virtually wrecked by a Ponzi scheme in 1996.

On the internet, the MLM model is widely used and accepted via *affiliate marketing*, which I shall discuss briefly in Chapter 12.

Offline, setting up MLM businesses is a job for seasoned professionals: our model entrepreneurs should not consider it. Online, Seb and Maggie will need to look at affiliate marketing for their website.

Large strategic allies

More useful for most new businesses is the right strategic ally. In this section we will consider 'large' strategic allies. Is there someone out there, with established market presence, who can help you get to market quicker, or to access a bigger market, or give you instant credibility in a market – or all three?

A classic example of this is Tom Hunter, now Sir Tom, who founded Sports Division. He persuaded a big

Glasgow department store to let him have a small space to sell his range of sports gear. In return, he promised to brighten the place up and get some PR.

Other examples can be found in the excellent book *Marketing Judo* by John Barnes and Richard Richardson. The point of the judo metaphor is that the art is not just to use your own energy but to harness your opponent's energy to your ends. (Like most metaphors, this one breaks down if taken too far: in business, you are using the energy of your strategic ally not to defeat the ally but to defeat your rivals.)

There are three magic words in the business of finding and keeping large strategic allies: mutuality, trust and empathy.

Mutuality refers to our old friend 'the win–win outcome', one of the few terms in managementese that I like. OK, you will benefit massively from the chance to promote your products to Megacorp's huge customer base, but what's in it for them? If there is no gain for the other party, the deal won't work.

Don't just assume that because you are small there is no mutuality – Sir Tom delivered on his promise to brighten up the big store and to do PR, and it really helped. Generally, 'being seen to help small business' is good PR for large businesses, who have, sadly quite rightly, acquired a bad name for the way they treat small suppliers.

Trust is essential. Act on your intuition when you first meet potential partners. If you don't trust them, move on. If you do trust them, still build slowly. Where relevant, ensure that any copyright and other core IP (intellectual property) is protected before you set out. As the poet Robert Frost said, 'Good fences make good neighbours'. Start the co-operation with a pilot scheme, and watch the outcome carefully. If things look good and you want to develop the alliance, get lawyers involved to set up the deal – it's a lot cheaper than getting them in to unscramble an informal deal that goes wrong.

In a good strategic alliance, there is *empathy* between the players. At the most basic level, your people like their people and vice versa. Even if an alliance creates a real 'win–win' in theory and both sides are honest, it still won't fly if your people don't get on with their people. This may not be true for alliances between corporates, but if one party is a tribal, passion-driven start-up, the empathy must be there. Encourage interaction and be alert for conflict.

If things don't work out, disengage quickly and cleanly. If you have been mistreated, shun the overpowering desire to get your own back and instead get on with rebuilding your business. The best revenge is a successful enterprise.

In a way, all start-ups use this strategy, by finding early trial customers. Later on, your 'customer mentors' will effectively be strategic allies. Among our model businesses, JEBR are most clearly using this strategy.

Small strategic partners

Strategic relationships with big companies can put a small business on a dramatic growth path. Less spectacular, but of more interest to many slightly less ambitious smaller businesses, are alliances with other same-size players.

The easiest way is by *cross-referral*. Elspeth's customers, for example, will no doubt be interested in other kinds of therapy. If she can build relationships with masseuses, shiatsu practitioners, reflexologists and so on, she can start recommending them and they can start recommending her. She is setting up a *referral circle*. Clearly, these recommendations must be genuine – the circle will only be as strong as its weakest link, so she should take time to find the right people to cross-promote with.

Difficulties can occur with a referral circle:

★ If a member's standards start dropping, action will have to be taken. Initially, it means a word in that person's ear. Ultimately, if they don't shape up, if means exclusion from the circle. Someone in the circle needs to take responsibility for this.

★ It can happen that one person gives a lot more referrals than they receive. This person needs to discuss this with the other circle members, rather than sit and brood on it. A circle leader is useful here: he or she can take an objective view. In the end, if the person is unhappy, they can always leave. Often, these things self-adjust over time.

★ I've heard people argue that these circles lose you business. This can happen. Elspeth recommends a reflexologist; the client goes, is delighted, and says, 'I'm not having aromatherapy any longer.' However, this effect is minor compared with the extra business that a referral circle can bring. And even in this case, Elspeth will retain the goodwill of the lost client, who may well send any of his or her friends who are interested in aromatherapy to her.

It is usually best if the circle operates on the principle of trust rather than by referral payments. In some industries, people expect formal affiliate programmes (more on these later), but not here.

Business exchange organisations such as BNI or BRE are effectively referral circles for business-to-business enterprises. I will talk more about these in the section on networking (see p.100)

If there is a business with whom you have a special rapport, then you can take this further and do actual *cross-promotion*. Elspeth could offer a half-price aromatherapy session to customers of her friend Bethany, who is a reflexologist. In return, Bethany will offer half-price reflexology to Elspeth's customers. This is a nice win all round for everyone.

Similar to this is the case where small businesses *co-operate* to create a new, larger product to offer to the public or to a large buyer that might not be interested in a small solo business. If Mark has a friend who is a self-employed accountant, and this person knows a self-employed HR consultant and a marketing consultant, maybe all four could band together to offer a 'Small Business Doctor' service.

Small businesses can also co-operate in promotional work, to raise general awareness of an area of business. Elspeth and her circle could organise a 'Holistic Health Fair' at the local town hall. Should she invite Bill, a rival aroma-therapist, to participate? Some people say no, he's competition; but as long as Elspeth likes and trusts Bill and believes that Bill will be a help in organising the event, then I think she should. If Bill won't help much but will spend the whole fair trying to draw custom away from Elspeth, then it's not such a brilliant idea.

On a more general level, don't forget that even your rivals have common interests with you. In a very ruthless business, this may be downplayed, but it's still true. For example, a rival may recommend a supplier, not just out of benevolence but because they value the supplier and want to be seen to be bringing them business. (I've never heard of anyone recommending a particularly bad supplier in order to drive newcomers out of the market, though I'm sure it can happen!) Sometimes competitors are clearly on the same side, for example when facing a legal challenge to the basis of their business (as in the food supplement industry in 2004–5) or in the face of rising rates of government interference and taxation.

There is a kind of Darwinian myth that business is all about ruthless competition, every individual continuously slugging it out with every other individual. At the other end of the spectrum, some people try to make out that business is really very cuddly, about being happy, making customers happy and even being lovely to the competition, because we're all in the same boat, really, aren't we? At Beermat we tend towards the latter approach, but understand that there is always a balancing act, a line to be drawn between Darwin's savannah and Cosmic Marketplace Oneness. Every individual business person has to work out where that line is for them: it depends on you and your style of business.

Your business plan

The above strategic considerations should be thought through before you write your first business plan – which you should now do.

From a marketing perspective (and from others, too), this plan is still provisional. You know you have products, and you think you have the right products. You think you have the right target market. You have thought through the issue of intermediaries, and maybe signed one or more up. It's certainly time to write some kind of plan, but do so with the awareness that things will change: this plan is not a nice, clear 'road map'.

Business plans are often compared to road maps, but this analogy is flawed. Armed with a road map I can get from Lowestoft to Aberystwyth, because there is an existing road network out there which the map tells me about.

There is no existing network out there leading direct to your business goal. The world out there is perpetually changing, and you become part of that change the moment you set up in business.

This is particularly true of an early, provisional business plan, so be prepared to make alterations to it. And to write another, much better and clearer plan in six months' time.

Actually, you may not have to rewrite the whole plan. A business plan is usefully thought of as two entities. The first is a kind of 'constitution', which lays out the values and purpose of the business. Who are we? What is our way of doing things? The second is about 'numbers'. The former should be pretty invariable, but the latter will need to change as you learn and grow.

The overall topic of writing the business plan is covered in many books (including, of course, *Finance on a Beermat*), so I won't go into it in any depth here. However, as a marketer, you should note that...

★ your plan should begin with your elevator/party pitch form, filled in.

★ there should be a specific marketing section of the plan, which should contain:

• an outline of your products, their specification and price

• the routes to market for each of these products

• specific sales targets for each product

- your estimate of the average cost of acquiring a customer

- your estimate of the five-year value of a customer

- specific marketing projects planned, and what you are budgeting for them

- specific targets for each project.

Clearly, any substantial strategic alliances should be discussed in the introduction to the plan, and the marketing aspects of these should be covered in the marketing section.

Take-off strategies

* ★ Routes to market
  * Direct selling to customers (recommended for most businesses)
  * Subcontracting
  * Agents, distributors and resellers
  * Franchising, MLM, licensing etc.

* ★ Strategic alliances with large companies
  * Seek mutuality, trust, empathy
  * Build slowly: pilot first

* ★ Strategic alliances with same-size companies
  * Cross-referral
  * Cross-promotion
  * Co-operation on products or promotion

* ★ Time to draw up a provisional business plan

www.beermat.biz

Chapter Eight: Informal Marketing

This chapter is all about what I call 'informal marketing'. It covers topics such as networking, word of mouth and generating referrals. These are not covered in 'Big Marketing' books, but are essential for the new and small business.

These topics do, of course, overlap with the topic of sales. I apologise if any *Beermat* fans get that feeling of *déjà vu* (or *déjà lu*, I suppose, in a book), but I'd rather have it that way than miss out this important material.

Big Marketing assumes a big budget. You do not have that. You do have other resources, however: yourself, your creativity, your social skills, some time. Put these to work in the service of your business.

Networking

Successful business people are usually excellent networkers. This is especially true in small business – you can rise to the top of a corporate by being an invisible accounting genius, but such a person will not build a great business services company (unless they have a brilliant sales cornerstone). So get out there and network.

As with all marketing, your networking should be planned, targeted and assessed. Networking isn't just about going to endless social events talking about what you do. It's about attending specific business-related events. At some of these, you will be asked to make a brief pitch. At others, it will be a matter of circulating in a room, talking to people as if at a party.

Business exchange events

At these, delegates stand up and give a brief pitch for their business. Naturally, you should have yours ready, but in practice I find that the first time you make it is always an experiment, and that you hone down what you really need to say over a few live pitches. The mirror is a good place to get rid of the worst tics and non sequiturs, but there is no substitute for an actual audience to give you that gut feel for whether you are saying the right stuff or not.

There are a number of business exchange organisations to choose from. The best known national ones are BNI and BRE. BNI has a strict rule of 'one trade per chapter' (a 'chapter' is a local group), so if there is already a web designer in Harminder and Jat's local chapter they are out of luck. BRE has different rules. Find out about other national organisations. 4Networking has been recommended to me as pleasant and unstuffy (and doesn't insist on one trade per chapter). If you prefer to network by phone, contact Ozone (www.ozoneconferencing.com). This group also has regular offline meetings.

There will also be local networking groups to explore.

Talk to other business people about what's available in your area, and see which ones they recommend. The big national organisations vary hugely from chapter to chapter. The bad chapters do too much hard selling and not enough referring; you are always being badgered to bring along new members, and at the same time no real leads emerge because the outfit is actually run by the local Mafia, who aren't interested in giving business to uppity newcomers like you. The good chapters are friendly and welcoming, and create a real circle of value creation, where members help each other out. I know of one freelance programmer who got £15,000 worth of business from his first year in BRE. For solitary entrepreneurs, good chapters can also provide the company of like-minded people.

The only way to know whether your chapter is a good one or not is to turn up, experience it and, most important of all, trust your instinct. If you get a nice feeling and want to get involved, it's a great way to build your business. If you don't, head politely for the exit.

Naturally, these organisations are of most use to businesses that sell to other small business. Harminder and Jat should definitely try this method (especially the more outgoing Jat), as they may find clients sitting in the room, as well as referrals. Mark should do the same. Elspeth? If she fancies it, she should give it a try, but I would suggest she treats this as a specific niche market and develop some stories about how stressed business owners benefited from a nice relaxing therapy session.

Other business networks

Other networking organisations do not require you to pitch, they just create a place and a time for people to meet, after which it's up to you. Check out your local chamber of commerce as a start.

There are also online networking groups, such as ecademy or LinkedIn. I shall discuss these in Chapter 11.

Networking techniques

For some people, networking sounds hell, but if you are a lone business-starter, you have to get out there and do it. Here are some hints.

Traditionally, we were taught it was rude to speak briefly to people then move on. But at networking events people are there to meet as many people as possible, so this rule is counterproductive. Instead the rule-breakers are the ones who try to monopolise others. Skimming round the room is not a sign of superficiality but what everyone is there to do. Speed-dating is often used as an analogy: participants only have three minutes to make an impression on the other person, then someone bangs a gong and everyone has to move on. Apparently it works pretty well: we all have powerful intuitive skills, and make up our minds incredibly quickly about whether we 'click' with someone.

And it is about 'clicking'. As the old adage has it, 'people buy from people'. People do business with people. This is particularly true in the world of small business – though even JEBR are more likely to find co-development customers among people who like them as individuals (it will change once they get selling to early adopters...).

Do some preparation. You may be able to find out some info on who's going to be there. If so, make a shortlist of people you want to meet. If you can find out what their interests are, think of a 'conversation opener'.

You will soon find that your instinct has kicked in, and you either like this person or not. If you don't click, move on. If you do click – move on, too. You have other people to meet. In both cases disengage politely: swap cards; explain that you're here to meet as many people as you can; if there is something that you know you will want to contact that person about soon, say so.

Don't be bound by your 'shopping list'. If you feel drawn to someone who looked irrelevant on paper, go with that feeling.

Next morning, make notes on the back of business cards. Or, even better, have a filing system with boxes to tick – did you click?; what subject of common interest did you find?; how did you leave things? Then follow up the people you liked. (If this all sounds too cold, rethink. Business is about people, but it is also about being businesslike.)

In speed-dating, if the attraction is only one-way, the introduction is not effected. In the less structured world of networking, you are bound to get follow-ups from people you didn't like. Have another think about them; if you still think 'no' – well, it's up to you. Not to reply is probably less rude than being inauthentic and false-polite or being actually rude.

If you contact someone and they don't reply give it another try, as emails can get deleted by accident or just get de-prioritised on a busy day. If you still get nowhere, back off. You'll probably meet them again, and maybe this time you'll click. Don't hound people. If you feel you are being hounded, send a polite email answering any specific questions but making it clear you are busy. Maybe they would like a brief chat at the next networking session… In the meantime, remember to lock up your pet rabbit.

The need to network has upset traditional social etiquette, but has not turned social gatherings into free-for-alls. New rules apply, which guard the integrity of the individual while allowing for more interaction. Follow them, and enjoy the experience.

The sector community

You will need to be a member of this. You may wish to join the relevant trade body, but even if you don't, there is a way in which you can informally belong to the community. You will have already started reading the trade press as part of your intelligence-gathering. If an article strikes you as absolutely spot-on (and about time someone said this!) or complete and utter rubbish – write to the editor. A measured tone rather than a rant is best. (If you feel very strongly, write the letter, but don't send it for a couple of days.)

The trade press will announce trade shows and other events. Attend these. Not everyone will be conversational at trade shows, but some will.

The aim here is not to make sales, but to get an ever better 'feel' for your market: how it works, where it's going, who 'makes waves', and generally what you need to do to achieve success.

Word of mouth

Why is J.K. Rowling one of the richest women on the planet? Because her publishers spent a fortune on marketing? No. Because people loved her books, and told their friends about them, who loved the books and told *their* friends, and so on…

Word of mouth is the best way to sell any product. The reasons are obvious: we're all used to being bombarded by ads, PR etc., and while these still have a use, they don't carry nearly as much weight as the recommendation of someone we know, like and trust.

Of course, just because of that, word of mouth is beyond our control. However, we can do our best to get it going and to help it along. After that, the product is on its own out there.

If you make something good or provide a good service, you will acquire *evangelists*, people who go round telling their friends about you. This is what J.K. had, by the million. If you have such people, make sure you reward them. Not financially, which is the worst way, but by giving them a special treat. Take them out for a meal. Offer them a free gift. You probably know them, so you'll know what kind of gift would hit the mark.

Some people don't feel easy about being praised, and are secretly embarrassed by their own evangelists. If you are in this category, you must get over this. Most of us lug round psychological baggage from our early life, much of which might have been useful when we were three and a half but which is not so for us as adults. For many people this includes beliefs that they are not really allowed to be successful, or that successful people are flash, dishonest or have achieved success at the expense of others. It can also involve powerful self-deprecation, along with which comes the belief that anyone who says anything nice about them is only flattering them.

Many readers will look at this and think: how silly, I'm not like that at all. Lucky you. Many others will relate to it. If that is you, then it's time to go to a coach and get these issues sorted, as they will otherwise dog your business career.

I've quoted Malcolm Gladwell's *The Tipping Point* before, but the book does need a mention here. It made a study of how word of mouth spreads, and identified the key participants as 'mavens, connectors and salesmen'.

'Mavens' are a special kind of evangelist. They are people who become experts on narrow topics, and to whom other people turn for advice. I have a friend in the village where I live who's an expert on wine; not a paid expert – he doesn't have a wine column in the papers or anything like that – but if I need a recommendation, I give him a call. Your local business community will have people like this who are happy to be consulted informally by others.

Naturally, mavens make up their own mind about things, and value their independence. You can't buy or charm your way to their recommendation. The best you can do is make sure that they know about your product and know about it in the best light (without being too pushy). After that, it's up to them.

'Connectors' are people who naturally build networks. Again, you probably know people like this – naturally gregarious individuals who often give parties and enjoy introducing people. 'You must meet X...'

Get to meet connectors, and if they like you, they will 'network you' with other people. Sometimes these links aren't that useful – connectors can be a bit indiscriminate – but at other times they can be of huge value. Remember to thank the connector for the contact: they like to be appreciated. And keep in touch with them: connectors are often so busy connecting that they forget you, but are usually delighted to hear from old contacts and do another round of connecting. If you can, accept any invitations to events they invite you to, unless there is a huge price tag attached.

'Salesmen' can mean not just professional sellers but any-one with a knack of persuading others to do or buy something; and they can also be female, so the term isn't a very good one. Maybe 'persuaders' would be a better term, except that for people of a certain generation, Tony Curtis and Roger Moore will immediately leap to mind.

In Gladwell's model, the mavens pick up on a piece of information. They are part of a network run by connectors, through which they spread the word. Salesmen are also part of the network, and will pick up on the word and convince other people to use it.

Is this how things actually work? Up to a point. I've met mavens and connectors, but not many 'salesmen' as defined by Gladwell. All the salesmen and -women I have met have been professional salespeople working either for specific companies or for themselves, rather than just hanging around waiting for something to promote. But mavens and connectors certainly exist and are of huge use. Find them, cultivate them, and be your own salesperson or get someone to be your 'sales cornerstone'.

Big-company marketers, especially those selling to young people, are now putting a lot of effort into *viral marketing*. This term gets used in two ways. One is 'any attempt to get word of mouth going about your products'. This is clearly something every business should aspire to. The second meaning is more specific. You make a video or sound clip that is brief and arresting (amusing or one which plays some kind of trick on the viewer), put it on sites like YouTube, tell as many people as you can about it, and hope it will 'go viral' – that it will be arresting enough for people to want to pass it on to their friends. Note that the quality of the production does not need to be anything special – as long as it's in focus and audible, you're OK.

A brilliant example of viral marketing is Richard Wiseman's Card Colour Experiment (do try it: www.quirkology.com). It's short, simple, memorable and, beneath it all, says rather a lot about how we blunder through life with our eyes closed. This clip quickly became the most viewed on YouTube and has clearly promoted the author's site and his books.

However, most small businesses don't deal in such arresting stuff. Dull, worthy clips won't get circulated. Vulgar, over-the-top clips may get circulated, but is that the message you want to send about your business? (If the answer is 'yes', then don't let me stop you!)

Stealth marketing techniques include paying actors to pretend to be consumers using the product in a conspicuous way, submitting fake customer reviews to websites, putting marketing messages into the mouths of fictional people in discussion groups or phoney blogs ('flogging'), and setting up fake pressure groups that appear to be driven by public concern (called 'astroturfing', because such groups often pretend to represent 'grass roots' opinion). Much of this is both dodgy and beyond the resources of the start-up or small business.

There is, of course, a more traditional way of getting a 'buzz' going about a product – PR (more on this in the next chapter).

Customer mentors

This is a concept that Mike Southon and I developed in *Sales on a Beermat*, but it needs restating here.

Once your business is up and running, the best evangelists possible are your existing customers. If they like your work or product, they should be happy to provide endorsements and referrals, as well as other useful stuff like honest feedback on your products and their delivery.

Looking at these more closely…

★ *Endorsements* ('I used this product and it's great!' says Fred Bloggs of Acme Industries) are useful back-ups to marketing materials. These can be written testimonials, or the more general permission to 'use my name' when promoting a product. Particularly nice is the specific promise: 'I'd be happy to endorse your product – if someone's in doubt, they can call me.'

★ *Referrals* are even more valuable – a personal recommendation of your product to another potential customer. Many business owners are scared to ask for these, thinking it a bit of a cheek, but many customers actively enjoy giving referrals – once they know, like and trust you. So when your intuition tells you that they do feel this way about you, ask.

When asking for any of these, if the customer seems uneasy, don't push. It represents a commitment for them: effectively they are putting their reputation on the line for you. They may want time to consider. If they say no, or, more likely, something like 'I can't think of anyone to refer you to at the moment', then let it go. Someone else will say yes.

Endorsements and referrals are of huge value to new and small businesses. David Frey, author of the *Small Business Marketing Bible,* says that 45% of service businesses are chosen not because of formal marketing, but on the recommendation of respected third parties.

Informal marketing

Networking
* Business exchange events

  • Best for businesses selling to small business

  • Go with your instinct – chapters vary

* Other networks, including online groups

* The sector community

Word of mouth
* Evangelists, mavens and connectors

* Viral marketing

* Stealth marketing

Customer mentors
* Endorsements

* Referrals

Chapter Nine: **Make Some Noise!**

This chapter is about public relations, or 'PR' – working with the media to gain positive coverage for your business. People have become pretty cynical about PR. It is equated with 'spin', with deceitful politicians and multinationals, with 'sexing up' dossiers and so on. And it's expensive, too. Surely it's all part of the big-business marketing armoury that small businesses are better off without?…

No. PR, when used intelligently and with the marketing mindset (in other words, respect for the intelligence of the customer), can be a powerful tool for generating 'buzz' and business. And it can cost you nothing but time and imagination.

In writing this chapter, I've been hugely helped by Louise Third, who is the best small-business PR person I know. She wrote our ebook *PR on a Beermat* and runs a company, Integra Communications Limited, which specialises in helping small businesses make some noise in an already crowded, noisy world.

Which is what PR is all about.

Of course, your noise has to obey the basic laws of marketing communication, and be the right noise, aimed at the right people, and followed up by measurement.

Clearly, some businesses are more 'PR-able' than others. Clothes with a Conscience is a PR person's dream. It has a message that resonates with modern sensibilities. There will be a continual drip-feed of stories of how a particular line was sourced, of how Seb and Maggie found a particular supplier who refuses to use child labour and so on... The shop is a physical space, so events can be held there, which will create 'news'.

Also some businesses need PR more than others. As a general rule, consumer businesses need PR more than 'b2b' ones – but see the comments on JEBR below.

Seb and Maggie both need PR and are highly PR-worthy. A happy coincidence. The question facing them is should they go straight for hiring a PR agent, or should they do it themselves? Arguably, they should go for the agent, as they will have enough work cut out running the business. But that would make this section of the book rather dull, so I shall assume their budget does not run to that, and that they have decided to do their own PR to start with. Once the business is up and clearly generating reasonable streams of cash, they really should get a specialist in.

All other businesses of this type – restaurants, hotels, venues etc. – need PR. But oddly enough, so do JEBR. This may seem strange, as they are about as unlike Seb and Maggie's clothes shop as a business could be. What does it matter to them that Joe and Joanna Public know about them and their highly sophisticated technical product? The answer is, of course, that it doesn't; but they have a different, and equally pressing, PR requirement. Remember that for them a crucial issue is credibility. The right kind of PR, targeted at the right media – specialist press, trade events, even academic papers – will be of huge help to them. Given this market, they should be quite easy to PR, as they have genuinely interesting new technology.

Elspeth is, like Seb and Maggie, selling to the public too, so PR will be of great help to her. The media love health issues, so she will have plenty of opportunity for creating PR if she follows the advice below.

Mark, Harminder and Jat, selling to SMEs, are probably less in need of PR, which is just as well, as their business is harder to PR. But they can still make the right noise in the right place and benefit from it. I believe strongly that:

★ There is no business that cannot create some PR if its owner/manager is imaginative.

★ PR will always help their business.

There are four basic principles of PR:

1. Target

2. Be realistic

3. Create news

4. Measure.

Target

Early in the life of the idea you settled on a target market for the business. This might have changed in the light of early sales, but as long as it is still clearly defined, then that's fine. You know who you need to be talking to.

Then you need to know how to talk to them. Find out what media your target audience takes notice of. The easiest way to find this out is simply to ask them. At the same time, do a little reconnaissance: for business customers, what publications do they have lying around in their reception? You should be reading the trade press anyway – their trade, remember, as well as yours. If yours is a local business, as most start-ups are, then read the local paper and listen to local radio.

Be realistic

Certain types of entrepreneur dream of being splashed across national dailies or appearing on *News at Ten*, which is fine – dream on, but don't waste valuable resources of time, influence and effort on bringing this about. Trade and local media are *much* more suitable targets than national. They are more targeted and they are much, much easier to talk to.

Create news

This skill lies at the heart of good PR, and can be done in many different ways – see below.

Measure

It is not easy to measure the effects of PR, but you must try. Keep asking, 'And how did you get to hear of us?' You won't get 100% reliable answers, but you will see trends. Keep asking customers and potential customers if they have seen media coverage. Collect media cuttings. You can get mileage out of these, too – once you have ten or fifteen pieces, put the folder (or a copy of it, anyway) in reception. It will impress visitors.

News

This is what PR, for the small business, is about. But what is news, exactly? The answer is anything happening, or simply being said, that will interest people.

News can be made, or rather, ordinary events can be made news, by using imagination. I'm not talking about massive hype here; the art of small-business PR is turning relatively mundane events into something quirky and intriguing enough to attract a little attention from your target market.

These small packets of 'a little attention' will build into awareness if enough of them are disseminated and taken heed of. PR is a cumulative activity. Any given piece of publicity will attract some people, but it is the overall effect of repeated mentions that creates awareness.

Your launch

A launch is the formal, public announcement that you are in business. The early 'deal' sales I talked about in the previous chapters come before the launch. You are now ready, with clear products, prices and positioning. 'On your marks; get set...' The launch of a business is a classic news opportunity.

Among our model businesses, Seb and Maggie's shop presents the best launch opportunity. The opening of new premises on the local high street will always attract some interest, and they have an especially interesting story to tell for theirs. If you are opening a high-street business with a less radical premise, don't despair – you can still make the event interesting. Think what would amuse your target market, and organise some kind of competition around it. It doesn't have to be very profound or challenging – it can be wacky things like seeing how many footballs you can stuff into a Mini, or raising money for charity by having a 24-hour jazz jam, or giving prizes for customers' children's drawings (make sure there's a tiny prize for every entrant)... What matters is that:

★ The local media will cover it.

★ People involved will have fun, which in turn sends out the right message to the public: you're not just a 'stuffed shirt' trying to make money out of people, but a likeable and engaged part of the community.

Free offers are less newsworthy, unless it's something like a free glass or three of champagne, which the reporter from the *Bugle* might be interested in.

For our other, non-retail businesses, the launch is less newsworthy. However, the local and/or trade press might be interested in the 'story behind the business' – which is essentially about the founder(s) and why he, she or they are starting up. Story does mean story! (See the section on press releases – p.125 – for more on this.) A basic rule is that *no business launch should occur unnoticed by its intended target market.*

Once your business is launched, how can you keep up media interest? The answer is 'in as many ways as you can imagine'.

Events

Our two consumer businesses can always stage special events to attract media and public interest. Seb and Maggie's shop is an ideal venue; Elspeth may have to hire a room. As with all marketing, the events must follow the rule of saying what you want to say to the people you want to say it to. But within those limits, you are bounded only by your imagination.

Elspeth could give displays of essential oils. She should prepare a talk on how aromatherapy works and its history. Neither of these two need involve much cost apart from her time: the displays could be at craft or mind, body, spirit fairs (she should be able to wangle a free stall if she gives a talk). The talk could be given to WIs or civic societies.

Seb and Maggie might want to set up a special charity to help producers in poor countries and have fund-raising events for it. Some people may be cynical about this, but as long as Seb and Maggie aren't cynical, their integrity will shine through to enough people. They could also have displays of traditional crafts in their shop, or talks about the countries where the clothes come from. The list is endless.

Don't despise special designated time-periods. Some of these are rather wacky, like Compost Awareness Week (in May); others, like World Aids Day (1 Dec), are serious. If you can hook an event to one of the major days/weeks/months, then do so – the media loves them. There is a list at www.projectbritain.com.

Whatever you do, make sure that you get as much media coverage as possible. This won't be much for a talk to a WI – but even so, make sure the local paper gets a release about the talk. And clear this with the person who invited you.

Stunts

These work well for some consumer businesses, not for others. If you want to walk down the high street dressed as a chicken to publicise your new fast-food outlet, do so. Don't forget to have leaflets to hand out, with an offer on. If Elspeth were really confident she could cure a specific malady better than a conventional doctor, she could issue a challenge – but she *must* be confident of the outcome first!

Surveys

Once you have a customer base of some size (or can gain access to one), a survey can often throw up titbits of information. How often have we read news items along the lines of 'According to a survey by XYZ Ltd, people eat four times more sausages than they drink pints of beer'?

Our business-to-business enterprises can make noise here. Can Harminder and Jat find out some odd piece of information about the internet? Almost undoubtedly. This would be excellent PR, and might also be marketing intelligence. Mark is a smaller business, but if he could find out some information about how much small-business time is wasted on badly managed projects, he would have good material for the trade press (and, again, valuable intelligence for his marketing).

The trick is to have a hunch that some counterintuitive fact (and one that is relevant to your business) is true, then go out and test it. There are a number of online survey tools available, the best known of which is probably SurveyMonkey (www.surveymonkey.com).

Case studies

I've already talked about these, but must mention them again here, as they are excellent material for the trade press once your business is up and running. Remember: beginning, middle, end. A customer with a really tricky problem; a particularly neat solution (which demonstrates your USP).

Awards

This is a great route to recognition, especially for small business-to-business enterprises. It's easy to be dismissive of these – do the Middleshire Chamber of Commerce annual Enterprise Awards really mean anything? The answer is, yes, in the Middleshire business community. Even entering gets you noticed by someone, and if you make it through to the finals, you get into a catalogue and, most important of all, get coverage in the local business media.

Entering awards is also good for the business. As part of the submission process, the company gets to look at itself as if from outside, as do the staff, who usually end up wiser and happier about what the company is really for. And if nothing else, if you get into the finals, there's a nice evening out.

I think people become cynical about awards because winners overuse them in their PR. 'We won such and such an award…' said in a rather superior way invites the reply, 'So what?' It's no substitute for good products or a compelling USP, but we know that. Awards help with credibility.

As with all these PR tools, make full use of it. The award giver will provide a bit of PR, but you can and should provide a whole lot more.

Sponsorship

This isn't just for big companies: £100 for a local prize can get you started. The keys to getting this right are to find the right 'fit' – sponsor something that really reinforces what you are trying to say about your business, rather than a sports event that the boss happens to enjoy – and to keep control of the process by entering into a clear contract with those you are supporting.

Here is Louise's checklist for your sponsorship agreement:

★ specify the amount of money or help-in-kind being given

★ specify the duration

★ agree how the funding will be applied

★ agree all the detailed extras such as guest tickets, speaking slots, use of logos, press releases, etc.

Most important of all, you must ensure that you get media coverage for your sponsorship.

None of our model companies are ideal for sponsorship. It's probably a bit too big a deal for the one-person companies. Seb and Maggie already have their charity, and should probably put their sponsorship effort into that. Harminder and Jat might, when they are bigger, use this tool, for example if they find all their work is within the Sikh community or with a particular industry sector, but this is essentially a business-to-consumer tool. Of course, when they get big, JEBR should pursue this route, sponsoring brilliant students to highlight their own academic excellence (and hopefully ensuring at least some of the students subsequently join them). But just because this tool isn't ideal for five of our model businesses, that doesn't mean it won't suit you.

Talks

This works best with consumer businesses. Our clothing-shop owners will have endless stories about their trips abroad to source clothes. They must work them into a talk and tell them!

Elspeth is already giving talks. And given that he is a bit of an extrovert and a natural speaker, Jat might well raise their profile and pick up business with a talk. 'How to design websites using open source tools' probably won't get the crowds in, but maybe a talk on 'Great internet disasters and how to avoid them' would work.

Press releases

All the above must be supported with a press release. As with much PR, there is a lot of cynicism about these. Some of this is justified – a lot of press releases just aren't interesting. They are written because someone has been told to do one, and duly get churned out, without any imagination or thought for what editors want. Which, of course, is material which will please their readers, either by informing them, or entertaining them, or, ideally, both.

A strong press release is snappy and to the point. One page of A4, typed with 1.5 line spacing, is ideal. It should, of course, be relevant to that editor and that publication. It should also, of course, be properly written, with correct grammar and punctuation – editors have been schooled in this stuff and care about it, and will be unimpressed by poor English, unless the story is of outstanding interest. Leave time for the editor to factor a piece into his or her plans: local papers like a couple of weeks' notice of an event; trade magazines are usually monthly and will have longer lead-times – some as long as three months.

Ideally, the release tells a story. Here's Elspeth's launch release, done by a friend who's 'done a bit of writing' and who got a book out of the library on how to write press releases.

New therapy practice in Middletown

Elspeth Scott has a Level 3 Diploma in aromatherapy, which she gained at Middletown College of Further Education. She is also trained to level 2 in massage.

She is now offering aromatherapy treatment for a range of problems including migraines, depression and skin and joint diseases.

She says: 'I want to create the best possible experience for my customers.'

Contact her on…

Yawn. Who cares about the first paragraph, apart from Elspeth's mum and her tutor at the college? At last, we get some meat in the next para, though precious little. The quote is bland – doesn't every business say that?

Yet the release has kept to a good rule (keep it brief) and is written to a correct formula (see below).

Luckily, she has another friend who works in PR, who came up with the following:

New treatment for migraine, depression and skin disease – and it works!

A new treatment for migraine, depression and skin and joint disease will be available in Middletown from 1st January. It will be given by Elspeth Scott, a qualified aromatherapy practitioner.

Elspeth was originally a sceptic about complementary therapy. But in 2003, a friend of hers developed a rash on her upper arm, which proved resistant to all sorts of standard medical treatments. One day, this friend told Elspeth she was going to try aromatherapy. After six sessions, the rash had gone.

Elspeth was so impressed that she signed on at the local college, at first for an introductory course, then for the full, three-year diploma. Now she is qualified, and is determined to spread the benefits of this system of healing to as many people as possible, through her new business, which will operate from her home in Brompton Street.

She says: 'A lot of people think that aromatherapy is just some nice smells, plus a bit of relaxation. It is that, of course, but it's also much more. Did you know that aromatherapy was used to treat gangrene on soldiers injured in World War Two?'

Contact Elspeth on…

This isn't going to push the latest disaster or scandal off the front of the nationals – forget images of cigar-chewing editors in shirtsleeves shouting 'Hold the front page! A woman has opened an aromatherapy practice in Middletown!' – but it will attract local attention. People don't like to hear boasting, but they are hugely interested in genuine stories of other people, how they came to be doing what they are doing, what their passions are and any unusual (or even moderately unusual) chains of events.

Mark, Harminder and Jat probably won't have such interesting stories, but there must be something objectively interesting about them. Let's assume that they have not led hugely eventful lives. Even so, Mark has a new product idea, and should talk to the trade press, like *Small Business Adviser*, about it. Harminder and Jat have the least original product – there are plenty of website designers around – but can they get a piece about their new business in the local Sikh community newsletter, or even Jat's cricket club newsletter? Can they make their launch more newsworthy by designing a simple website for free for a local charity?

A basic format for press releases is:

★ Header. Something that will grab the editor's attention.

★ 1st section. A paragraph of basic factual information.

★ 2nd section. Expand on the basic facts. Can be more than one para if necessary.

★ 3rd section. A quote.

★ 4th section. A contact name and phone number.

If you have a decent photograph, aesthetically pleasing, on-message and of sufficient quality (300 dpi or more), that will add greatly to the effect.

However well written the release, it can still fail, if you don't *follow it up*. For most people this is harder to do than writing a release. But it has to be done. Editors are used to being followed up, and don't mind as long as it is done authoritatively but politely. Leave a while (a week is about right) for the release to arrive, then ring. It's perfectly OK to say, 'I'm just checking to see if my press release arrived.' If the answer is no, then offer to resend. If yes, ask them if they think there was a story in it. If they say no, ask what sort of things they are looking for. Always, always, always be polite.

Writing feature articles and newsletters

A *feature* article is essentially any article that isn't news. Classic examples are 'how to' or 'comment' pieces. Can you write these? The trade press is eager for well-written feature pieces. If you can become an established voice in your trade magazine it will raise your profile considerably.

Clearly, the more you read the magazine, the more you will get a feel for its house style – or, if it's any good, styles. A good magazine will have both serious and lighter news and features.

You must be honest about your writing ability. If you are in any doubt, find a professional writer and pay them to write the piece. A badly written piece will ensure that the editor does not deal with you again in the future, or, if it does sneak into the publication due to sleepy editing, will reflect badly on your business.

Over time, of course, you can develop your writing skills. I used to write all the Beermat materials, but Mike Southon now writes his own column for a major national paper.

In the long run, your aim is to be on good terms with the editors of your local paper's business section and the relevant trade magazines, so that when you have an idea for a feature, you can just call them up and chat about it.

Starting off, however, your approach to editors needs to be a little more formal. First of all, think through the idea. Check that it really is right for the publication. Then prepare an elevator pitch of the piece – a brief summary of what you are saying and why it is new, challenging and of interest to that set of readers. Then contact the editor, and find out how and when they like to be contacted. (*How*, because some people like the phone, others email; *when*, because there will be times when an edition is being finalised, when they don't want to be disturbed.)

It may happen that they want to talk about the idea straight away, which is why you should get your elevator pitch right first. More likely they will suggest a time. It is also possible that they will say no, they source all their material from professional journalists – in which case, you need to find out which journalists they use, get in touch with the journalists direct and talk about the idea with them.

If they want an email, make it brief. Include the elevator pitch, add that you could write the story up in full, and ask how many words they would like. When they give you a figure, please stick to it. Editors have specific spaces to fill, and hate receiving pieces from contributors that don't fit.

If they prefer to be contacted by phone, then make that call! Don't be pushy – simply say that you have a story that might interest them, and tell them the potted version. The editor will either say 'no thanks' or pursue the story. Often the latter means asking you to send them a slightly longer summary by email.

Once you have sent your full version in, wait. If you hear nothing for a fortnight, chase politely.

With both features and press releases, never forget two things:

★ The bad news. Editors are often bombarded with material, so yours must stand out.

★ The good news. Editors have space to fill, every week or month. As an active participant in your sector, you are the sort of person they want to hear from. If you can produce relevant, entertaining, well-thought-through and well-written material, they need you.

Newsletters are really for larger businesses. Both the preparation and sending them out can be costly – but they are well targeted and they do keep your name in the customer's eye. Some basic rules:

★ Keep them snappy.

★ Keep the marketing mindset and 'think customer'.

★ If you have time, make them interactive. Have competitions, ask for customer stories etc.

★ Start small and build up if you get positive feedback from recipients. A newsletter that starts with a big fanfare then suddenly vanishes sends out a very bad message. Bear this in mind when producing the first edition, which will be an exciting thing to do and which will make you come up with loads of good ideas. Have you got the time to do this every month?

Maybe the days of the paper newsletter are over – many newsletters are delivered via the internet. I shall discuss online PR in Chapters 11 and 12.

Allocating time and money

You can do most of the above work yourself – so it should cost the business nothing!

If you are a consumer business, you should set aside a morning or an afternoon a week for it. If you are 'business-to-business', PR is probably less important to you, so trim this figure, but don't spurn PR altogether. To get the maximum value out of this time, get a PR coach – Louise offers such a service: contact her at www.integracommunications.co.uk.

In practice, a small budget is advisable for things like a decent photograph of yourself or (for the shop) of the premises, professional writing (if necessary) and maybe a lunch with an editor you find you click with.

Taking on professional PR

If you do decide this is right for you, then take your time choosing an agent. You should choose someone:

★ whose work you admire

★ with whom you 'click' personally

★ whom you know (or believe) to have good contacts in the media in which you want to feature

★ who provides you with at least two references.

The more of your own PR you have done, the better able you will be to make the right choice, and to provide a clear brief for the agency once you have taken them on.

Many small business owners get really 'into' doing their own PR. They enjoy it, and find that the contacts they make are good sources of intelligence about their markets.

Make some noise!

* ★ You can do this yourself
* ★ Basic rules
  * • Target
  * • Be realistic
  * • Create news
  * • Measure

* ★ News can be...
  * • Your launch
  * • Events
  * • Stunts
  * • Surveys
  * • Case studies
  * • Awards
  * • Sponsorship
  * • Talks

* ★ Contacting the media
  * • Get to know editors
  * • Be patient and polite

* ★ Allocate time – and money

www.beermat.biz

Chapter Ten: Other Traditional Marketing Tools

I'd like to begin this chapter with some comments about branding, then discuss specific media such as ads and brochures. The new, exciting world of online marketing I shall leave to the next chapters.

Branding

To many marketers, this is the very heart of the subject. Huge tomes get written about it. However, I feel it should be taken down a peg or two. Not lots of pegs, but a couple. For many small businesses, branding is not nearly as important as *reputation*. Branding clearly does matter, and the start-up should think carefully about it, but in the end, all the branding in the world won't save a poorly thought-through and poorly delivered business, while many excellent businesses continue to delight their customers and duly prosper without giving a thought to branding. This is particularly true for business-to-business service companies.

What exactly is branding? It is an attempt to encapsulate and communicate the essence of what is valuable (to the customer) about a business. Marketers call this essence your *brand identity*, and establishing it is the first task of branding.

What's yours?

The best way to answer this is to ask your customers. Tell them you're having one of these branding exercises, and ask them to suggest five adjectives that sum up the company and why they buy from it. Naturally, you'll get some jokey answers – if they're all jokey, then maybe that's your brand! – but also some more serious ones. If you ask enough people you will get enough serious answers to spot trends.

Hopefully, the answers you get will be the ones you expect, reflecting the vision of what you wanted the business to be like that you set out with. Beermat, for example, values the following:

★ clarity

★ simplicity

★ action (getting things done and learning by doing)

★ making work as much fun as possible

★ an ethical approach.

If our customers came back to us saying we were obscure, overcomplicated, purely theoretical, cold and dodgy, then we'd know we had an image problem.

The totally new company hasn't got customers to consult, of course, so has to think ahead about what it wants its customers to see and experience. Go back to your elevator pitch, and think about the pain you solve (how would the customers most like to have it solved?) and your USP.

Having established brand values, branding is about expressing those values through all possible media: visual, words, sound, and in the case of any business with premises, in the 'feel' of the premises. This is where you really do need professionals, people who understand the implicit vocabulary of their chosen medium because they work with it every day. Tell me what brand values you want to convey in words, and I'll do it, but don't ask me to select colours, design a logo or compose some suitable music (though I am not colour-blind, can draw and play the piano).

Rather than complain about the cost of branding, look on it as a rather magical process, where you tell someone about your business as you want your customers to see it, and they go away and paint a picture of it, or sum it up in sound.

The mystery of branding can, of course, lead to spectacular balls-ups. Small business owners don't know whether to laugh or cry when another £500,000 gets wasted on a big-organisation 'rebranding' which is clearly inept. (I tend to laugh if it's a corporate and cry if it's a government department – that was our money!) But this shouldn't put you off the exercise yourself.

Some hints:

★ The best people to tell you about your brand, as I've said, are your customers. So when you start up, brand provisionally. When you have enough customers to ask, you will not only have a much clearer idea of what your business is about but will also have a decent size sample.

★ If possible, do the above before you launch.

★ Don't be bamboozled by branding 'experts'. It's possible to get very metaphysical about branding very quickly. If you think the conversation is going over your head, go elsewhere. There are plenty of honest, straightforward, talented and commercially savvy designers about.

★ Remember that branding is essential for some businesses, and simply useful for others. (Cue sound of the Marketing Inquisition sharpening its instruments of torture: this is heresy!) Seb and Maggie *must* produce beautifully coherent and expressive branding for both their shop and their website. That doesn't necessarily mean the shop must look posh, but it must look exactly how they believe their customers will want it to look. JEBR must have excellent branding when they hit the 'early majority' market, so should start thinking about it now. Elspeth doesn't have to spend a fortune on branding, but should get her basics in place. Our two business-to-business entrepreneurs need to worry less about physical branding, but should have clear beliefs about the value they are offering customers (so why not do a little branding based on these beliefs?).

Remember: branding is about how your customers experience you, not what *you* see when you look in the mirror. Ideally these should be the same – but often they are not. I've seen companies 'brand' by just looking inward: it's all jolly good fun till the new brand is unveiled to the public, who fail to connect with it at all.

Branding will have a huge influence on the design and use of all the media discussed below.

Traditional marketing tools

Packaging

Packaging might seem to be one of the big-business aspects of marketing that this book is keen to avoid. Certainly many of the billions of US dollars spent on packaging worldwide come from big corporates. However, it is an issue all businesses need to think about. There are basically two aspects of packaging. One is what products need to protect them, keep them fresh etc. The second is what makes them appeal to buyers.

The Clothes with a Conscience online shop will need to consider how to send out its goods in a way that is safe but also not seen as wasteful (their customers will undoubtedly be ecologically aware). For the actual shop, the consideration is more about what buyers will use to take the clothes away that they have bought – something recyclable, but not dull and dowdy. The bag is an advert for the shop: in other words, this is part of its branding.

Elspeth should consider always wearing the same outfit when she goes to work with a client, or at least something distinctive, like a particular scarf.

Both the above are consumer businesses. Business-to-business companies, especially business-to-business service companies, might consider that this sort of stuff is irrelevant to them. It is not. Every business needs to consider the overall visual effect that customers and potential customers will associate with their product. Stephen King, co-author of *Finance on a Beermat*, is also a skilled marketer, and recalls working with a computer repair company who sent operatives to business customers dressed in – well, whatever the repair person fancied wearing that day. He told the company to insist on a simple uniform, just a sweatshirt with a logo, and was able to raise prices by 30%.

Adverts

I won't go as far as to say that traditional advertising is an aspect of big-business marketing that small businesses can ignore – but I'd like to sow that thought in your minds, and then retreat from it a little.

Certainly, PR and 'informal marketing' are much more powerful tools than advertising for most small businesses. However, ads do have their use. My feeling is that adverts are best for special, one-off events, especially those that are difficult to PR, like a sale or special offer – though even here, a voice in my head is objecting, 'Can't you *try* and PR them? Tie in an event or a talk or *something*…'

'Advertising is a soft option,' says Graham Michelli. 'Think of other ways of attracting attention, and you will end up doing a much better, more personalised and locally relevant piece of market communication.'

If you must advertise, there are rules:

* ★ target

* ★ have something to say

* ★ tell a story

* ★ test.

Target local press and relevant trade media.

By 'have something to say', I mean don't go in for 'Coo-ee advertising'. Always drive home your USP. Include some kind of offer in an advert, for instance, '5% off with this ad', 'Free dessert with this ad', or 'Free bottle of essential oil with this coupon'.

By 'tell a story' I'm stretching the metaphor a bit. I mean: lead the reader through a process that begins with their taking notice of the ad and ends with them taking some kind of action that connects them with you. That process has a beginning, a middle and an end, so I'm going to call it a story.

There are numerous acronyms for how this story should be told. The first one I learnt was AIDA, and I've not really found a better one. It oversimplifies a bit, but it is pronounceable and captures the essentials, so I like it.

Attention. This is the job of the heading, the most important piece of copy in the ad. A good heading 'selects the right audience and promises a benefit' (to quote the classic book on writing ads, John Caples' *Tested Advertising Methods*). Elspeth might try 'Skin problems? Try this new therapy that works or your money back.' This is not a clever heading. People without skin problems might even think it's a bit naff. But people for whom this is a pain will be attracted and respond. Great small–business ads don't win awards at posh adland dinners, they get business.

Interest. This is essentially proof – evidence – that the product works and that you can deliver it. 'This stuff works!'

Desire is aroused by driving home the relevance of your solution to the reader. 'This stuff will work *for you*!' A special offer should be included to make the product even more desirable.

Action. Always end with a call to action. Phone this number now. Cut out this coupon and send it to…

Small ads can be very useful marketing tools. They don't have the space to do all the above. Get attention with a headline. State your offer. Require an action of the customer. Bam! Short, sweet, cheap and often effective.

Like all marketing communication, you should test your ads as ruthlessly as you can. You may think you've written a brilliant ad, but if it doesn't pull in business, then it has failed – at least in the publication in which it appears. It might work brilliantly in another publication. This testing can involve a lot of work.

Arguably the most important thing to remember is that if you find a formula that works (a particular ad in a particular place in a particular publication), *stick to it*. One golden rule of marketing is that you will get tired of your marketing materials long before the public does. Resist the temptation to change a successful ad just because 'it looks a bit old hat'. The public will tell you when it thinks it's time to change.

However, as I said, many businesses don't really need to do much traditional advertising. Seb and Maggie should advertise their launch and any special offers. Elspeth should try small ads in local and subject-specific media and see what works. Harminder, Jat and Mark? I cannot see a great deal of value in their advertising, and there is certainly none for JEBR.

There is a problem here. I've talked a lot about getting free PR in trade and local media, and am now saying that advertising is not a particularly effective way of getting business for many businesses. But these media rely on advertising to survive. If everybody pulled their ads and just went down the free PR route, the publications would probably disappear. There's no easy answer to this, but...

★ Up to a point, that's business. You can't avoid doing what's best for you just because some other business might suffer.

★ If you do strike up a good relationship with an editor and they publish a number of your pieces, and then they ask you to place an ad (especially if there's a good deal on offer) – well, why not? Monitor the ad, and if it fails, you can say so next time they ask you to put one in. Remember, you are after a win–win outcome over time.

Sales letters

These work best for businesses with broad targets, such as charities. (People selling credit cards, 'collectables' and rather dodgy 'good luck' charms seem to rely on them as well.) However, the Beermat recommendation is to find a narrow target and hit it hard. If you can get a really gilt-edged list of names and addresses of people who clearly fit smack into the middle of your target market, then send them a sales letter. Otherwise, other media are more efficient.

If in doubt, write assuming the reader has pain of the kind you solve. Those that don't will bin the letter, feel a little aggrieved, then forget all about you. Those with the pain will be amazed at your perspicacity.

Make sure there's a real offer in the letter. 'Coo-ee sales letters' are even more wasteful than 'coo-ee advertising'.

And don't expect magical levels of response. Even top sales-letter writers expect low response rates from them: around 1% is regarded as pretty successful. If you assume each letter costs 40p to prepare and send, then that means you're paying £40 for each response. Is that good value? You should be able to do better with Google AdWords (see p.179).

The basic aim of sales-letter writing is the same as ad writing – to move the reader from attention to action. There are innumerable templates online for sales letters – just Google 'sales letters' and you'll get loads of them, all saying largely the same thing. The key to using them wisely is to adjust them to your audience. Sophisticated buyers will be infuriated by attempts to 'inject scarcity' ('There are only seven days left to take up this amazing offer…'); strings of 'PS's look unsubtle, too.

There's a debate about whether you should send sales letters or postcards. Postcards are probably best for quick reminders to existing customers; sales letters give you the time and space to really convince people that they need what you provide.

Brochures

Arguably nobody needs printed brochures any longer – have an electronic one online instead. You can update it whenever you want; people can access it whenever they want.

However, it's useful to have something to leave behind after a sales visit. In that spirit, our business-to-business entrepreneurs should have cheap, simple 'leave-behinds' prepared once they have launched. The design should be in keeping with the branding, and the content should be a simple statement of the elevator pitch (the pain you solve, who for, how you do it, why you're special, your credibility).

The leave-behind must not become a substitute for the salesperson talking the prospect through their pain and exactly how your company will solve that pain and why your solution offers particular value. No salesperson should be allowed to say, 'It's in the brochure.'

Leaflets

If one of the key benefits you offer your customers is that you are local, then a leaflet through the door of every house (or business, if you're 'b2b') in the area is an excellent piece of marketing. (It works less well in cities where people live in flats, and tend to sort mail into 'for me' and 'everything else'.) You can get leaflets printed cheaply. Keep them simple. Follow AIDA. Highlight your USP ('At last, a Thai restaurant in Middletown!'), and make an offer ('5% off with this leaflet').

Seb and Maggie might try several leaflet 'drops' in different parts of Midchester. Each 'drop' should involve a leaflet with a unique reference number on it and make the offer conditional on the leaflet being produced. This then becomes an exercise in marketing intelligence as well as communication.

Exhibitions and trade shows

JEBR will need to start attending these. Initially, they probably just turned up as visitors, but as part of their drive to build brand recognition and 'look the part', they will have to take a small booth.

This will be costly, so they must set crystal-clear objectives and work towards them. These could be very precise. Maybe there are five buyers from five multinationals they need to talk to. Then everything they do should be aimed at making that happen and making it happen as pleasantly and effectively as possible. Invite the five people to lunch or dinner, offer inducements for them to visit the stand – whatever it takes, as long as it's legal...

At the other end of the scale, Elspeth will be exhibiting at Mind, Body, Spirit fairs. The same rule applies. Her aims will be less precise, but she should set numerical targets: sign up 10 new customers, hand out 100 flyers, get 25 business cards (with permission to email donors), do 2 interviews, sell £50 worth of essential oils...

Being an exhibitor at a fair or show creates PR opportunities. Louise Third says: 'There may well be a special edition of the top trade magazine being issued especially for the event – make sure the organiser's press office help you get featured in this, via an article or interview. (This will need planning at least two months in advance.) The organisers should also have made a big effort to get the relevant press along to the exhibition. On the day, make sure the organisers' press office gives you the names of all the editors and journalists who are there. Track them down.

'You should also negotiate a speaking slot. Most exhibitions run seminars or workshops to keep visitor interest and add value to their attendance. The topics vary from technical to inspirational, but are all well attended by exhibition visitors eager to take a break from traipsing round stands and to learn something new.'

Shows can be great marketing opportunities, but can degenerate into expensive rituals if allowed to. 'We have to be there every year. It's a bit of drag, really, but the boss says it's all about brand.' Large businesses can't afford to be so unfocused, let alone small ones.

Marketing from premises

For Seb and Maggie – and anyone else selling to the public from premises – the premises are themselves a marketing tool. For a shop, the window is the first point of contact with the passing public. Get this set up by a trained window-dresser. People opening shops often think they can do this themselves – and they can. Anyone can, but not to a professional standard. Finding window-dressers is easy: put an ad in the local paper – 'Part-time window-dresser required. Good rates of pay' – and you should get replies. Get the dresser to redo the window for each promotion, but have him or her come in every Friday to make adjustments depending on how the promo is going.

Always price goods in the window. This sounds obvious, but it's amazing how often shops fail to do this. No price, and customers assume that you're somehow ashamed of the price, and that if they go in there'll be a whole lot of trickery to get them to part with more money than the item is worth. Instead, be proud of your price. Yes, this *is* worth £59.99. Then let customers make their own minds up.

Customers will be passing the shop all the time, and they need regularly to be offered new inducements to come in and buy. Retailers soon get used to living in approximately six-week cycles, created by their annual trading calendar. Some of these cycles are determined by the season: January sales, spring, summer, autumn and winter specials, Christmas… Others need to be special promotions, which for Seb and Maggie should be easy: Indonesia, Nepal, Peru, wherever they get their clothing from.

Each promo should have a 'lead product', something you think will sell particularly well, and which is then given a competitive price.

The theme should be expressed throughout the store, not just in the window. Put up pictures of daffs for your spring promo, pictures of Aztec pyramids and smiling locals for your Mexico month, and don the Santa hats in December. Reorganise the layout of the shop for each promo, with the lead product at the front, other aspects of the promotion next, then standard goods at the back. As with goods in the window, make sure everything is clearly and confidently priced. Add extra information, especially about unusual items such as the special Mexican clothes – anything that will make the customer think, 'I'll try one of those…'

Promote each promotion. Hand out flyers, email your database and have some kind of launch, to which the local press (and your regulars) are invited. For example, a Mexican food evening for the start of that promo. Enjoy these events, and the guests will too. Don't oversell at them; if the event is in the shop, your layout and the goods themselves should do that.

Above all, the premises must look interesting and buzzy. Bored staff filing their nails or lurking behind tills reading magazines will not create this effect — the buzz must start with them, which means it starts with you, the owner/manager.

There's loads more to 'space management' — Seb and Maggie went on a course to learn about it — but more important than any of this is *flair*, which people either have or lack (though they can acquire it over time). Flair for choosing a great lead product; flair for making a shop look, feel and be inviting; flair for inspiring staff with genuine enthusiasm for your products and customers.

Other 'premises-based' businesses do not have the opportunities that Seb and Maggie have, but should never forget:

★ Your premises are a key part of your brand.

★ The premises must look and feel alive, confident, attractive, interesting.

Customer service

This is sometimes regarded as not a marketing issue, but something to do with admin or general management. This is not the case. It is an essential part of how you market your business. The smile on the face of the shop assistant is marketing. The tone of voice of the person who answers the phone is marketing; so is the fact that the phone always gets answered – sign up to a service like AllDayPA unless you are permanently by the phone.

If you have the marketing mindset, then both the design and implementation of customer service will come naturally to you. Sadly, to some entrepreneurs and small-business owner/managers it does not. Be honest here. If you are at your happiest helping a customer solve a problem, then you have the mindset. If other things give you more of a buzz – making money, being an expert, getting stuff done, working with a great bunch of people – then you need someone on your team who does have the mindset. You can set up formal systems for customer service, but in a small business these will never make the difference that an individual with a genuine marketing mindset will.

Sadly, I see many examples of rubbish customer service. Even more sadly, many of them are in the small-business sector. If you are a small-business owner/manager, please take note of this. You can't beat the big boys at marketing budgets, power over suppliers, access to cheap finance, ability to lobby government and so on, but you *can* beat them on customer service. Hands down.

This is especially true in retail. Imagine a high street suffering from competition from a big supermarket on the outskirts of town. Time for local retailers to get together and remind everyone that they have both more time and more expertise than the supermarket checkout staff. But instead, the shopper encounters a patchwork of customer service. Some is very good. Others… Mr Jones takes an item to Anytown Electrical to be repaired, and is told that it is a cheap one so it serves him right that it conked out. Mrs Jones goes to Anytown Kitchens and asks for a recommendation on a washing machine, and is simply told what they have in stock. Little Emily Jones goes to Anytown Shoes and is told they don't sell children's shoes.

People without the marketing mindset will say that the shop owners were probably busy that day, or have just had terrible news, or are generally depressed by the effects of the supermarket. But to a marketer that is a fundamental rule of business broken, as dumb as not doing your accounts or perpetually selling products for less than they cost you to buy.

So be friendly and respectful to your customers. Smile! I know that sounds corny, and that a forced smile is probably worse than a neutral expression. But you should be glad to see a customer. They keep you in business.

Traditional marketing tools

* **Branding**
    * A visual or aural metaphor for your business
    * Get a professional
    * Especially important for consumer businesses (must be memorable) . . .
    * . . . Or for businesses selling to corporates (must look credible)

* **Classic tools**
    * Packaging
    * Adverts
    * Sales letters
    * Brochures
    * Leaflets
    * Exhibitions and trade shows

* **Retail**
    * Premises are a marketing tool
    * Regular promotions
    * Space management plus flair

* **Customer service**
    * Communicate your values
    * Be friendly and respectful

www.beermat.biz

Chapter Eleven: **Marketing Online – the Basics**

The internet offers both amazing new opportunities and new techniques for marketing, especially for the small but ambitious business, which can now both broaden its scope to engage with customers all over the world and at the same time narrow down its market into ever more precisely defined niches. You can combine the global reach of a multinational with the precision of a specialist...

...If that is what you want to achieve. The net, like all marketing tools, works differently for different businesses. The key to using it does not necessarily lie in mastering the latest piece of fancy software or getting on the latest social networking site; it lies in knowing what your business needs from the net and making sure the net delivers that.

In this chapter I shall look at the basic online marketing tools, and in the next one at the more sophisticated ones.

Your website

Every up-and-running business should have a website. The question is, what sort of website? We have already looked at a very basic kind, which is the right place to start for most businesses, but it's time to move on. Where to? How far?

There are two main reasons why people visit small-business websites. One is that they have heard of you and want to check you out. The other is that they are surfing the net in search of an answer to a problem.

So your site's first, most basic, function will still be as an online *brochure* to reassure the first type of visitor that you are real professionals. Some small businesses may not need to proceed beyond this stage, especially if they are not selling particularly innovative products and do ordinary, 'offline' marketing well.

However, even at this basic stage, can you find a pleasant way of getting hold of people's names and email addresses so you can build a database? I say 'pleasant' because I click away from sites that want my contact details before they'll say anything other than 'hello' and 'let me sell you something'. Write an ebook about what you do, and give it away as a gift in return for these details and permission to keep emailing people (you will have to send a follow-up email checking that the person really does want to hear from you – your web designer will provide the exact format).

The next step is to create an online *information provider*, with 'how-to' articles by yourself and your people (including, if he or she is willing, your mentor) for the second type of visitor, the surfer in search of a solution. This visitor may just be curious, or they may have real pain of the kind you solve. Assume the latter, and close your pieces with a sell – I prefer a subtle one, but you know your market.

Next, your site can become a *magazine*, where the content is more wide-ranging. What are the trends in your industry? What do you and your people think of them? This will give you extra credibility with both sets of visitors, as well as attracting a third kind: those who particularly like your site and visit specifically to see what you are up to.

Beyond this, you can become a *club*, with interactive features like quizzes, competitions, and Question and Answer pages. More sophisticated online clubs charge for membership, but you have to offer something very special in order to get money from online club members. Start with a simple 'name plus email address' membership requirement, then build.

Seb and Maggie, of course, are going further still, and are building a site that is a *shop*.

The ultimate aspiration is, perhaps, a *portal*, a site that people use to access thousands of other sites. To create such a thing is very expensive, and to discuss it is beyond the scope of a small-business guide like this.

Where do our model businesses fit on this scale?

All Elspeth needs is a simple brochure site. She could also add information: hers is an unusual subject that people want to know about. If she really gets into the web, then she could try a blog and a few more formal 'thoughts about the industry' pieces. But she should only do this if she really likes doing these, and mustn't take her eye off the ball: her main marketing will be through referral circles, promotion and simply talking to people.

H and J have the resources to build a great site, but that can also be a danger – will a new feature actually create extra value for them? A really nice brochure site, with excellent case studies, would actually be enough. Endless discussions about the state of the web industry would probably not interest customers.

Mark Tait needs to educate the market about what he does, so should provide both information and industry comment. The catch for him is that he also has a limited budget. He has decided to start simple, with an online brochure plus a simple detail capture, and move up the ladder as he gets established.

JEBR should have an elegant site that helps them meet their principal aim, that of establishing credibility with corporates. Academic papers and case studies of successful co-development projects should feature.

Seb and Maggie, of course, must take online marketing to a different level to make a success of their online shop. In the next chapter, I shall take a brief look at the tools they will be using – but my main advice to them is don't build an online shop on your own; get a pro to help you.

If all you need is an online brochure, or an information provider, you can design and build your own site.

However, for any business with any ambition, this is a false economy. You'll be networking to get business; use this medium to give some business to a fellow SME like H and J, and get a pro job done. Your time is better spent on other aspects of building your business.

Nevertheless, the more you understand what makes a good site, the more you will be able to get value out of your web designer, so here are some pointers.

★ The site should be *logical*: easy to navigate round, with clear categories. It should be uncluttered and easy to read. Don't use a plethora of fonts; stick to classics like Arial or Verdana (good for screen reading).

★ A pretty standard *format* for web-pages has evolved, with a 'masthead' (heading) at the top, navigation bars down the left-hand side and/or along the top of the main text, and a secondary bar with duller things like terms and conditions along the bottom. Stick with this. And don't make the page too wide: people hate 'scrolling' horizontally.

★ Remember that many of your visitors will be using laptops or old computers with low-resolution screens. Test your site by changing your screen settings to 800 x 600 resolution. If it looks good with those settings then it should look fine on most computers. Also, don't forget to check it works with different 'browsers', including the increasingly popular Firefox (you can get a free download from http://www.mozilla-europe.org/en/products/firefox/).

Web copy

You must get your web copy right. Visuals and layout are important, but in the end it's the written word that convinces site visitors. Here are some hints:

★ Every page should have a 'headline', to grab the attention of the click-happy surfer. These should be simple and factual, not clever.

★ Use short sentences and short paragraphs. Have space between the paragraphs.

★ Use frequent sub-headings in the text. Many online readers are impatient, and 'skim-read'.

★ Use highlighted words – but don't overload your text with them. One or two per paragraph is ideal. Note: hyperlinks (those blue underlined words you click on that take you automatically to another page) can double as highlighted words.

★ Use bullet points.

★ Keep text to one page, except for articles which can be as long as they need to be. Research shows that many online readers don't scroll down pages. (Some people disagree with this: much 'pure' internet marketing relies on long texts. These are very sales-y sites, written to formulae. If you are going to follow the formula, then do so – it's carefully designed to keep readers engaged. If you're not following one of these formulae, keep the text short.)

A good online brochure for an up-and-running business should include the following *content*:

★ Home page. Simple, informative, eye-catching and, above all, quick to download. Avoid fancy intro pages – or anyone who tries to sell you one.

★ About us. The elevator pitch, plus a couple of your favourite customer endorsements. A picture of yourself.

★ Our products/our services. (If you are a service business, use the word 'service'. I use the word 'product' for goods or services in this book, but people arriving on your site might not.) Basic descriptions of what your products or services do and what they cost, plus the facility to click through to...

★ Our stories. Relevant case studies.

★ Our people. Have pictures of your team: people buy from people.

★ FAQs. Frequently asked questions – and your answers to them. These should help people through the buying process, and also overcome any fears or doubts that customers might have.

★ Links. A page of links to sites that you really think will help your site visitors.

★ Where we are. A clear map, please, ideally with written instructions added.

★ Contact us. Address, phone number, your name, an email form. List a standard 'geographical' phone number – it is more reassuring (people can check where it is) – as well as a freephone one.

★ Terms and conditions, and other legal items.

If you're creating an information source, add:

★ The Mycompany Ltd guide to… Tips and tricks aimed at people in your target market seeking information. Don't forget to brand the pages and ensure your name appears in the text.

★ Our thoughts. Your people's comments about the industry. Make these of real interest and value to visitors, rather than just consisting of a loud but discordant blast on your own trumpet. Imagine you have to get the material past an editor (or, better still, if you can afford it, get a journalist to be your editor).

You might also wish to include:

★ Blogs. (More on blogging below.)

★ 'What's new?' Information about upcoming industry events – including, of course, your own company and product information. Catch: this must be updated regularly. If you don't want to work on the site often, it is better not to have this feature, as few things make a site look sadder than 'hot news' that has gone cold.

Some thoughts on blogging…

Blogs are essentially one's diary or one's thoughts (or both) put up on the internet. (The word is short for 'weblog'.) Some commentators regard this as a great marketing opportunity, but I have yet to be convinced. Some people are natural bloggers – they lead particularly interesting lives, or they express themselves forcefully and in an original way. Fine, they should get blogging. But most of us lead moderately interesting lives and express ourselves competently but without magic. In other words, most of us aren't natural bloggers. Also, blogging isn't just as simple as biffing off a hundred words in an evening – successful bloggers have all sorts of strategies: posting on other sites, establishing links to your blog and so on. These all take time, which could be better spent on running your business. As an entrepreneur, your time is precious enough anyway.

Having said this, if you fancy blogging, go for it. Do try and exercise some editorial control – lots of sales talk or endless going on about oneself won't attract readers. I'd treat it as a hobby rather than serious marketing.

An interesting alternative to blogging is simply commenting on other blogs that you know to be popular. If your comments are fair-minded, intelligent and generally positive, then people will notice you. You will also be asked to leave a URL, which, although not visible to the reader, will enable them to click through to your site and will be noticed by the myriad-eyed Google.

A final, general point on sites – *keep your site maintained*. Check regularly to see all the links work and that all factual information on it is up to date. This might seem a rather trite point, but a recent survey, quoted by the Institute of Directors, said that 75% of the top 100 corporate websites in the UK had broken links and/or featured out-of-date information.

Website metrics

Measuring the effectiveness of your site is essential. There's no shortage of information – the difficulty is making sense of it all. If your site is professionally maintained by someone like H and J, then they should be able to explain this to you (though as with all these things, the more you know, the more intelligent questions you can ask).

People often boast about how many *hits* their site gets, but this is such a vague term as to be virtually meaningless. (It is always highly inflated, for various rather dull technical reasons.) The single most useful piece of information is the number of *unique visitors*. Unique visitors (or 'uniques') are the number of individuals who have visited the site in a given time period. If I visit my favourite site ten times, that is still only one 'unique'.

Other useful metrics are:

★ *Page impressions*. Every time someone clicks onto a page on your site, that is a page impression. So if someone visits ten pages on your site, that is ten page impressions. If ten people visit one page only, that is also ten page impressions.

★ *Visits* or *sessions*. Not to be confused with unique visitors. If I visit the site, that's a visit. If I visit twice, that's two visits. The number of visits divided by the number of uniques gives an indication of how 'sticky' your site is –

so if I have 1,000 unique visitors and 5,000 visits, that means on average every visitor has visited 5 times. Good news: they must have found my site interesting.

★ *Bounce rate*. This is the percentage of visitors who only visit one page on your site. Individual pages can also have bounce rates: the proportion of visitors who stay for less than a specified amount of time.

★ *Length of visit*. An average figure for all visitors.

★ *Referrer*. From what source did your visitors arrive? Google? Amazon? Your deadliest rival? This is useful when you are monitoring a new link you have set up.

★ *Your most popular pages*. Page impressions broken down page by page.

Your ISP should provide a free 'stats package', but these don't always provide all the information you need. Google have come up with a free tool called Google Analytics to help you keep track of your site and how it is working for you. This does, for free (unless you are a very busy site), the work of a program that a few years ago would have cost hundreds of pounds. If you are serious about online marketing, you should add this tool to your site from day one and invest time in working out how to get the best from it.

Email

One of the best marketing techniques for a small business is to build a database consisting of the email addresses of actual and potential customers. You can do this both online and offline. Online, make sure your site has a way of enticing people to part with their name and email address. Offline, collect business cards and be assiduous in putting the details into your database. Then use email to stay in touch with these people. Emails announcing new products are particularly successful – more so than emails announcing new offers, sales etc.

The next step up from this is to produce an e-newsletter. Print newsletters were essentially for larger businesses, but an online newsletter is easy to produce and disseminate. Get a professional to design a format, then send them out regularly. They do not have to be long: a 'thought' piece plus bits of relevant news is fine.

Email can also be used in the same way the post office was for sales letters – a tool for sending sales messages to people. (Unlike the post, recipients have to have given you permission to contact them.) This perhaps crosses the line between marketing and sales – see 'Mike's magic email' in *Sales on a Beermat*.

Other tools

Small businesses can raise their online profiles by participation in *online forums*, discussion groups and so on. This is really only worth doing if you enjoy this sort of thing – and can easily take up time that could be better spent elsewhere.

The same is true for *social networks*, a new marketing phenomenon. There are essentially two types.

* Networks aimed at any- and everyone, though in practice only used by people who are sufficiently internet-savvy. At time of writing, Facebook and YouTube are the major ones, with Second Life coming up fast on the rails (or floating off into outer space: choose your metaphor). If you are selling certain types of product – books, music, videos, especially those aimed at people under thirty-five – then you must get yourself onto these networks (or whatever replaces them). Your market is there, waiting to hear about you!

* Networks aimed at specific targets. Anyone in the business-to-business field should investigate ecademy, LinkedIn, or our own site for entrepreneurs (of all kinds, from lifestyle to 'the next Richard Branson'): www.beermat.biz.

Online networking isn't everyone's cup of tea. As I've said, if you're selling to the under thirty-fives, tough – you have to use these media. For other businesses, only do this if you enjoy it.

If you do enjoy online networking, remember:

* Your online connection is only the start. If you click with someone online, go offline and meet up with them as soon as you can.

* These sites all have an area where you place a profile of yourself. Make sure yours reflects your business, but

also your personal interests. Always include a photograph, and a link to your website where allowed.

★ It is only a means to an end – the growth of your business. If you want to let online networking take over your life, that's your choice, but your business will quietly fall apart as you do so.

Can you do *PR* online? If there is a site you particularly respect, and that you know your target market particularly respects, then approach them, asking them to feature your pieces or at least have a link to them. This will help your Google ranking (see p.171) and should get you noticed. Remember, however, that there is a lot of noise out there on the web: in my view, most 'offline' businesses still can't beat a piece in a top printed trade magazine.

Your press releases should also go out to the various free PR sites that exist (www.PRWeb.com is the best known). You won't get a huge number of readers, but it can't do any harm, and the links to your site will help your Google ranking.

Article marketing is when you submit short pieces (500 words is about right) to sites that automatically distribute material to a range of secondary sites. As with online PR, the articles should contain links back to your site, and this can help you on Google rankings. However, be aware that most article placements will be to crummy sites, like 'splogs' – sites that just stick on a load of random content then add ads, on which they hope to earn commission – for which Google doesn't have much respect.

Article marketing is a waste of energy for most small, offline businesses, but for online businesses, larger businesses or people seeking to be perceived as gurus, it can be of use.

The ideal outcome for a marketed article is that it strikes a chord with readers, who pass it on to their friends – in other words, it becomes a piece of viral marketing. However this is extremely rare.

eBay is an interesting route to market for small 'b2c' companies: not just the auctions, but the formal online shops you can open there. Many people run small, part-time and highly specialised businesses (often in 'collectables' or other second-hand goods) through these shops, and some of these build into larger, full-time and still highly specialised businesses. I must confess to not being an expert on eBay – people I know who use it say that the most important thing is to learn by doing: if you want to start an eBay shop, do some ordinary buying and selling first, build a reputation as an honest trader and at the same time get a 'feel' for eBay and the business style of its users.

More specific information on how to use eBay can be gained from the site itself or from the many specialist books on the subject. (Try the course on www.auctiontips.com/course.)

As I've said, small businesses need to be aware of the danger of becoming intoxicated with the internet and all the things it *could* or *might* do. It is foolish to ignore the net, but equally foolish to waste time pursuing endless fashionable 'hares'. Master a few tried-and-tested online marketing techniques – a quality site at the level you want it; a good system for capturing email addresses; keeping in touch with the people to whom those addresses belong.

Online marketing basics

* **Your website**

* **Web copy**
    * The most important aspect of your site
    * Keep it simple – short sentences and paragraphs
    * Use plenty of sub-headings
    * Keep text to one page per subject
    * Include the right content

* **Measure the effectiveness of your site**

* **Email**
    * Have a system for capturing names and email addresses
    * Use this to keep in touch with actual and potential customers
    * Do an e-newsletter if you have time

* **Other tools**
    * Social networking
    * Online PR
    * Article marketing
    * eBay

www.beermat.biz

Chapter Twelve: Specialist Internet Marketing Tools

Some businesses, of course, need to go deeper into internet marketing. In this chapter I shall take a very basic look at the more sophisticated techniques that specialist internet businesses use to attract visitors – or 'drive traffic', to use the buzz-phrase – to their sites.

Offline businesses with a brochure or information website should be aware of these techniques, though should be wary of spending much money on them. Seb and Maggie will, of course, have to be passionate about this material, and will have to spend money on it to ensure their online shop is well visited.

Search engine optimisation (SEO)

Everybody wants their site to be the one that comes up on the first page when someone enters their product into a search engine (Google, Yahoo, MSN etc.). You get this by giving your site a high ranking, or 'ranking high on Google'. There are two main tools for achieving this: links and keywords.

Links

Getting links to your site from quality sites is the single most important tool in SEO. It has a twofold benefit: the links are useful in themselves – people on these sites will follow them – and Google uses them to rank your site.

A while back, the rule for getting ranked was simple: the more links you had with other sites, the better. Now things have moved on; it's all about having the *right* links, i.e. links from sites that are regarded (by Google) as being both quality and relevant to what your site is about. A link from a 'splog' will largely be ignored, but a link from the premier site in your sector will help you in the rankings enormously. So make an effort to get the right quality sites to link to you.

★ Have content on your site (articles, case studies, blogs etc.) that is both good and relevant to the topic. That way, people will want to link to you.

★ Make a list of sites you want to be linked with, and approach them. Hint: pick up the phone and call the webmaster, who will be inundated by email requests for links.

★ Get your site listed on quality, relevant directories. Start with the Open Directory Project (www.dmoz.org).

★ Get your product or service reviewed on relevant sites.

★ Join debates.

★ Comment on the blogs of leading bloggers in your sector.

Online entrepreneur Peter Bennett recently launched a new site for Mandarin language training (www.mindynasty.co.uk). He says: 'The site had only been online since early December, and had a Google page rank of 0. In mid-December I searched for complementary but non-competing sites with high page rank. I found one (www.zhongwen.com) with a high ranking (6 – the max is 10, but 6 is good) and which I liked the look of. I picked up the phone and called the webmaster over in the US. I had a good chat with him about the content of his site, and asked him if he'd be prepared to link to me. I offered him a percentage of sales which resulted from visitors coming from his site, but he didn't want any money; he was happy to help a fellow enthusiast (perhaps surprisingly, many people are). The majority of the traffic we get to the site now comes via this link, and our Google traffic has gone from less than 10 hits a day to over 1,000 – and it's still only mid-January. This is all thanks to one link.'

He adds: 'Links are the online equivalent of judging people by the company they keep. If someone authoritative is prepared to link to you, then it's a vote of confidence in the quality of your site from someone who matters. Search engines recognise and reward this. The engines also like links because they are actually very hard to falsify. I control what I do on my site, so I could (if I wanted to) stuff pages with keywords, create huge sites automatically or employ other "black hat" techniques to fool the search engines. One thing I can't do is make changes to other peoples' sites.'

Keywords

Google uses these to assess the thematic unity and 'relevance' of a site. It also uses them as its basic search tool. If you enter something in the search box on Google or any other engine, it looks for sites with keywords that match.

Note that 'keyword' is not just used to describe individual words, but phrases or even complete sentences: 'cats' is a keyword, but so is 'Persian cats', and so is 'how do I look after my cat'.

Note also that there's a lack of clarity in the general use of terms. Technically, *keywords* are things found in websites, extracted by Google and used to match with *search terms*, which are what you and I type into Google when we're looking for something. However, the term keywords is now also used for what searchers type in.

Optimising your use of keywords breaks down into two topics: choosing the right keywords in the first place, and getting these onto your site in the right places, so the search engine knows what you are 'all about'.

Choosing the right keywords...

Your keywords – you need a collection of them, not just one – (usually) need to fulfil three criteria:

1. They accurately describe, or lead searchers to, your product.

2. They are the ones most used by people searching for your product.

3. They are a feature of as few other sites as possible (so searchers will find *your* site, not one of 1,000,000 others).

The obvious keyword for Harminder and Jat is 'web design'. That's what they do, and it's what someone looking for a web designer would probably put in Google. The problem is that Google then performs its utterly mind-boggling task of searching through billions of sites in just over a tenth of a second – and comes up with 'about' 369,000,000 entries for the two words. (If you narrow the search down and put the keyword in double inverted commas, Google will not look for just the word 'web' and the word 'design', but only the phrase 'web design' – and still comes up with over 250 million.) Condition three has not been met!

H and J should think about their segmentation. People often enter a geographic location in their search, so 'web design in Birmingham' will be a good keyword for them, as will 'web*site* design in Birmingham', and 'web design in West Midlands' – cover all the bases with your keywords. 'Web design for SMEs' would also help. As they have also 'segmented by pain', they should try 'Web design for new businesses' and 'Improve my website'. They should sit down and have a good brainstorm to see what they can add to these.

A remarkable tool to help you find and select keywords is www.wordtracker.com. This site monitors the search activity of the major search engines, noting down both all the keywords entered by anyone searching for anything *and* the number of sites that these keywords could land them on.

You start by entering a broad, generic keyword – the most generic one you can think of (e.g. 'biscuits'). Wordtracker will then build a 'matrix' around this lead keyword. Along the top of this matrix are 'related' keywords (garnered from other sites where your lead keyword is featured): for our biscuit searcher, it will come up with teatime, Garibaldi, gingerbread and so on. For each of these related keywords, wordtracker will then look in its index of hundreds of millions of searches, and find keywords (actually, phrases) which include that word – so for biscuits, it produces 'biscuit recipes' or 'buttermilk biscuits', for teatime it's 'kids' teatime', 'teatime treat' etc. From this matrix you can select the keywords you think are relevant, put them in a 'basket', then (here's the really clever bit) subject this basket of selected keywords to a test that will show:

★ how often each word is searched for

★ how many sites feature the keyword

★ a KEI (Keyword Effectiveness Index) ranking based on the first two pieces of information.

The ideal keyword meets criteria 2 and 3 on pp.174–5 above (lots of searchers but few sites) – and will have a high KEI ranking. This is much more useful information than just knowing how many times a search term is used.

If this all sounds a bit baffling, wordtracker offers a free trial: have a play on there, and it will soon make sense. The site also has a tutorial on: http://www.wordtracker.com /docs/ members_userguide/members_userguide.pdf.

If you are planning to take internet marketing at all seriously, then it's worth signing up properly for this tool.

Getting your keywords in the right place…

Having established a set of useful keywords, they need to be worked into the site so that search engines will find them and know that's what the site is about.

For all sites, there are various places where your keywords need to go.

★ In your domain name.

★ In your 'title tag'. This appears in two places. When you enter a term in Google and it comes up with a list, the title tags are the headings, in blue, of each site (so, for example, if you enter our publisher, Random House, the heading that comes up is 'Books at Random House'.) If you then click to that site, the title also appears in a blue bar across the top of the screen.

★ In your 'description meta tag'. These are the words which Google shows in black below the blue title entry. (For our publisher, this is 'Welcome to Random House, the biggest selling book publisher in the UK…')

★ In headings and sub-headings within the text.

★ Actually in the text itself. This used to be abused by people cramming text full of keywords, but Google now looks for an appropriate 'keyword density' (proportion of keywords to other words) in text.

★ Behind images. There are also things called 'alt tags' which go along with images and explain what the images are.

On more sophisticated sites, each page on the site will relate to, and be suffused with, a specific keyword – but this is not possible for many simpler sites.

In so far as your website is an online *brochure*, your most important keyword is your name. That is what people will enter if they want to check you are a proper business. If you have done the basics right – your name in the title tag, your name as the heading on the homepage, at least one mention on every page – your site should appear on the first page of the search, which is all you need. At the same time, employ other keywords that involve your products, to show Google that your site is relevant and focused – have a wordtracker brainstorm, but don't lose sleep over KEI.

When your site becomes an *information* site and/or a *magazine*, the battle for search engine rankings gets more complex – fun if you like this sort of thing, and expensive and exasperating if you don't. A top hint is that each page can have its own title and keywords, so a page on Elspeth's site discussing aromatherapy and traditional Chinese medicine could have those words and get a good ranking on Google, because there is little competition for the words (criterion 3).

Remember, for both links and keywords, the search engines are trying to make themselves as attractive to users as possible. They want everyone who searches for something (or clicks on an ad for something) to find sites that are respected in the sector and which are focused on that something. You want your site to be those things, too. SEO is often presented as a kind of battle between you and the engines, but actually, your interests are largely aligned.

One final word on SEO: it can take a while, often months, for these techniques to work. Don't expect your site to leap to number one at once. But never mind, as there is a way of getting searchers coming to your site at once. It is…

Pay-per-click advertising

I was pretty lukewarm about advertising as a traditional marketing medium, but in its newest form, pay-per-click (PPC) advertising, it is effective and beautifully easy to measure. The market leader in this is Google AdWords.

Enter any product into Google – I've just typed in 'ferries' – and you don't just get a list of websites. Instead you get a list plus:

★ above the list, a yellow box with some links in

★ to the right, a column of four-line adverts directing you to websites.

Both of these are called 'sponsored links' and are there because Google has been paid to put them there.

The principle is simple. These ads are triggered by the keyword (OK, technically 'search term') you entered. The advertiser pays for the right for this keyword to trigger this ad. More fully, they bid for the right for the keyword to trigger the ad in a particular position in the list of ads. Top of the list is often expensive; third or fourth is a lot cheaper. Serious buyers will undoubtedly click on more than one ad, so don't waste money bidding for the top slot.

The great thing about this system is that you only pay Google if someone clicks through to your site from the ad. If nobody clicks, the ad is free (and you've also learnt that that ad with that keyword doesn't work). Hence the name, pay-per-click. (There have been cases of unscrupulous rivals clicking on each others' ads, or even sending robotic clickers to do the job over and over again, but Google is getting wise to this.)

Google assigns every webpage in its index a 'quality score' by assessing its relevance to the theme of its content. If the page which you are advertising has a high quality score *and* if your advert matches the theme of the page, you don't have to bid so much to get the position you want on the list of ads. For example, if your page is all about products for new mums and your advert promotes a special offer on prams, you will pay less to get to the same position than a webmaster trying to promote a page with dozens of unrelated products. This really is an area where the small, smart entrepreneur can beat Big Money.

A big PPC campaign can get expensive, but you can start very cheaply, just running a single ad on an obvious keyword and see what happens. Google offer a special 'starter edition' for beginners.

As you develop, there are tools on AdWords to help you control your costs. Set a daily budget. You can tell Google you can only afford, say, £10 a day, and Google will keep your ad up until you hit that limit, after which the ad will disappear till next morning. Google even learns how quickly you get to this cut-off point, and will then make your ad appear for a bit, disappear, come back, disappear (and so on) in a way that spends your £10 evenly over the day rather than just putting up your ads as fast as possible until your budget is burnt.

You can run *campaigns* – you can create a number of ads, and Google will rotate them, noting down which ones get the best success rates.

You can run *local ads*, via an associated Google tool, Google Maps (enter 'pizza Cambridge' and you get three restaurants under a special heading 'local business results': click on these and you even get pictures of the restaurants).

You can have your *ad run on sites of a certain kind* (many sites now have a little section of 'Ads by Google'). This is via yet another Google service, AdSense. You can also use AdSense as an income stream if you don't mind other people's ads on your site. Google pays you for the space, not the advertisers. It's another neat idea.

I'm beginning to sound like an advert for Google, but this really is a very well-thought-out set of tools. As usual, the regular marketing caveats apply.

Keep monitoring your ads, checking which ones are getting clicks, and, more important, which ones are getting clicks *that then convert into sales*. It's relatively easy to monitor the click-through rate from ads, but on its own that isn't enough information. You have to find out which ads actually produce sales.

Set a budget and stick to it. If you don't do this, 'you might as well set fire to your wallet', to quote Richard Osborne, founder of Quick Formations. The budget must be based on the best assessment you can make of the value of a customer. 'You must ask "How much can we afford to buy a new customer?" and stick to that figure when planning and executing your campaign,' advises Ed Bussey, a founding member of the figleaves.com underwear retail website.

On its own, Google Ads won't bring in business. If the 'landing page' to which your ad directs respondents is ineffective, they'll just click away again. If the site behind it is poor quality, they'll do the same. Click – yawn – click; your money wasted.

Writing good Google ads

As with all marketing communications, think what you want the ad respondent to *do*. Buy something? Swap a free gift for their email address? Don't just bring them to your site, which is the internet version of coo-ee advertising.

You get four lines only – and one of these is a URL, on

which the visitor must click to get to your 'landing page'. Of the remaining three:

Line one is a heading. Make this as clear and action-oriented as possible. And brief – you only get 25 characters.

★ Learn about aromatherapy (Elspeth has produced a free ebook on the subject, which she will give in exchange for an email address and permission to email the recipient.)

★ Business website under £1K.

Mark tried 'Unblock your business', but this didn't work – it was too clever, too much of a slogan and not a clear enough statement of the benefit.

The next two lines are description. Think about your USP. And again, be brief; you only get 26 characters in each of these lines.

Among our businesses, only Seb and Maggie will need to run Google AdWords campaigns to drive traffic to their site. For the shop, it would be worth investigating Google Maps. For our other businesses, AdWords is a bit of an extravagance. But if the idea is irresistible (as it was for Elspeth, who's rather into the net)…

★ Remember – think what the ad is for. What do you want visitors to do?

★ Create a 'landing page' that encourages visitors to do this.

★ Sign up for the starter edition.

★ Find a good keyword (relevant to you but cheap to bid for).

★ Write a great four-line ad.

★ Bid for your ad to be third on the list.

★ Set a budget.

★ Go!

Before doing any of this, however, become familiar with the medium. Google some keywords around your subject and look at the ads there. Which ones do you think are good, and why? I also recommend spending some time on Google's 'learning center', at http://www.google.com /adwords/learningcenter.

Affiliate programs

Again, the principle is simple. Site A recommends its visitors to go to site B. Site B pays A for every visitor that follows this recommendation and buys something. Site A is an affiliate of site B.

This is big business: according to Wikipedia, £2.16 billion changed hands in the UK last year via online affiliate programs.

As with serious SEO and PPC ad campaigns, this is largely a game for big sites. As a small site, you can gain a little kudos by affiliating to big-brand names and thus getting their logo on your site. For example, many authors have sites where you can click through to Amazon and buy their books. However, you won't get much commission. The main reason authors use this service is because it means they can sell things without the hassle of running their own transactional site.

Seb and Maggie should certainly consider getting affiliates to drive traffic to their site. How should they do this?

★ Go looking for sites that would benefit from selling their product.

★ Email these sites and ask!

★ Know what a fair commission rate is. Commission rates vary massively from product to product. Affiliates can earn over half the price of a no-cost-to-produce, easy-to-download product like an ebook. Commission rates for large consumer goods will be 1% or so. Find out what the going rates are in your sector and match them.

SEO, PPC advertising and affiliate systems are the 'Big Three' of serious internet marketing, but remember that internet businesses should not become tech-snobs and despise ordinary marketing tools. Seb and Maggie will be using conventional tools (such as PR, leaflets etc.) for their shop, but even if they were running a pure internet business, it would still be worthwhile to:

★ Do conventional PR. A site can still be news in the real world! Figleaves did a lot of PR in the fashion press, and that brought visitors to the site. Richard Osborne entered (and won) a number of awards when starting Quick Formations.

★ Pay attention to branding and design. An online shop must be as well designed as a high-street shop would be.

'Pure' internet marketing

Seb and Maggie begin with a set of products, their ethically sourced clothes, and are using the net as a route to market. The purest form of internet marketers start with nothing but an open mind, a computer and a subscription to wordtracker. They then enter some generic keywords, build a matrix, fill a basket and check KEIs. What they are looking for is some clearly definable set of keywords with a really high KEI – in other words, a 'pain' about which a critical mass of people feel strongly enough to go searching for solutions, and a shortage of sites that provide those solutions.

This is an excellent way of doing market research, both into demand and supply, before considering realistically whether a business interests them, and whether they can actually make it work over the net.

It is a pretty inflexible rule for internet marketers that the more tightly targeted, or 'niche', the business the better. This plays to the strengths of the modern internet – its global reach, the ability of programs like wordtracker to examine search data in minute detail and the ability to design websites around specific keywords.

Pure internet marketers need to master many skills – the 'big three' above, the day-to-day mechanics of running an online shop, the writing of persuasive sales copy. One day, I'd like to write a book on the subject; here I have only been able to skim over the subject. Those wishing to pursue the matter further should go online for inspiration and information, where it exists aplenty (and is kept up to date). Be prepared to encounter a hard sell – but that's the world you are entering!

One word of warning: hardly a day goes by without some new technique, business model or piece of software being trumpeted to the pure internet marketing community. This means:

★ Perpetual change. You have to assess which of these myriad gizmos will actually add value, and, at the same time, which one of your tried and tested techniques has stopped working. Things can change fast on the internet.

★ Perpetual noise. Don't let the above become a distraction either from the day-to-day task of running your business or from your overall commitment to best marketing practice. Keep to the 'Ten Commandments' in Appendix C – especially number 5. Customers want real, solid benefits, not fancy features.

Advanced internet marketing

* ★ **Search engine optimisation**
* • Links

    With relevant, quality sites

* • Keywords

    Choose the right ones

    Brainstorm with wordtracker

    Put them in the right places on your site

* ★ **Pay-per-click advertising**
* • Understand the bidding process
* • Monitor costs
* • Write a good ad

* ★ **Affiliate programs**
* ★ **'Pure' internet marketing**
* • Research done through keywords
* • Evolving at great speed . . .
* • . . . So don't lose sight of the basics!

Conclusion

I hope that as you close this book you will take away an understanding of how important marketing thoughts and actions are for the new and/or small business, and how varied these thoughts and actions are. There can be no simple 'how you do marketing' rules – you have to select what is right for your business and your customers.

I hope also that you've enjoyed this journey with me. I find that marketing is a pleasing mixture of the disciplined and the creative, providing work for both the left and the right of the brain. Especially in small-business marketing, it has a technical side but it never gets too far away from people – more specifically, your customers: who they are, what they need, how you can help them.

I've hugely enjoyed the marketing I have done over the years, and hope you will too. If you hate it, you're probably not doing it right!

Finally, let's look at the outcomes for our model businesses.

H and J Website Design have not expanded – partly because they have not grown as fast as they wanted, and partly because when Harminder looked at the extra work that would be created by taking on staff, they decided instead to use 'associates', to whom they outsource work when things get too busy.

Their main marketing effort remains focused on reputation-building. Jat is a keen networker, attending several business clubs in his area; Harminder gets business, too, in a quieter way, through his family and faith community. They have not narrowed their market any further, finding work coming in from each of the three 'pains' they identified. They have followed my advice and 'upsold', selling ongoing maintenance/advice packages along with the original site-building contracts.

They spent a bit of money on a PPC advertising campaign, but it did not bring in much work. 'It just about broke even, and was hard work to monitor,' says Harminder. However, they don't regret having done it, as they now understand the system, and can add value to some of their clients by helping them with AdWords campaigns.

Mark Tait found the SME market difficult to crack, and in the end was hired back as a consultant by his old company, who have expanded up north again. 'I now do exactly the same job, but get paid better,' he says. Aware of the need to avoid being tied to one customer, he is planning to retarget his business at larger companies.

JEBR Technologies are still battling their way up the ladder. Many technology companies fail to appreciate the time it takes to build market presence – that Kevin Costner movie and its silly motto 'build it and they will come' still resonates in too many minds. JEBR never made this mistake, though they have found the cost of building market presence more than even they expected. As a result, extra outside investment has been needed – not an ideal solution, but both founders understand the need for it.

They have an impressive list of co-development clients, and are planning a launch next year, to the automotive industry, the sector in which they have found they deliver most benefit. They feel they have a fully rounded product, with bugs ironed out and a support system in place, and excellent testimonials from senior people in the industry, not just top techies. They are ready to go.

Elspeth Scott's PR efforts have had unexpected benefits, as she discovered a talent for writing and speaking, and now writes columns for the local paper and a national alternative health magazine. Her talk is also popular. Of course, these pay badly, but as a 'name' in the local health world, she can sell higher-value products than just a set of therapy sessions. She also works with three other alternative health practitioners to offer a 'complete health package', and has recently started targeting local business buyers with a 'stress-busting' product. The latter was originally aimed at directors, but is actually proving most popular as an incentive tool for female salespeople: moral, let the market tell you what it really wants.

The Clothes with a Conscience shop is bucking the current negative trend in retail, and doing good business. 'Marketing has been at the heart of our success,' says Maggie, who has clearly got flair for making the shop an interesting and fun place to be.

Their website has been less successful. 'The shop has magic – the moment people walk in, they get what we are about, and buy accordingly,' says Maggie. 'We never quite managed to capture that on the site – and, to be honest, we got so busy that we stopped trying to get both right.' The site is now more a brochure for the shop. Maggie's cousin is interested in coming on board to revamp the site, so maybe it will enter another phase – but Seb has an idea for expanding the shop into the site next door, which is soon to become vacant, and adding a café, so money for the website will probably not be available.

For all of our model businesses, their marketing journey continues.

Appendix A: Inventors and Marketing

Most inventors shouldn't market their inventions.

That will upset a lot of readers, but I'm not trying to stir – I just believe it to be true. Some people, like James Dyson, manage to be great inventors and great marketers, but many inventors lack marketing skills and are better off inventing more things and letting someone else do the marketing. There's no shame in this.

The big question is: who should do your marketing? There are agencies out there who claim to help inventors market their products. Some are reputable, but sadly some aren't. I had a neighbour who was always inventing gadgets and getting ripped off by agencies who said they would market them, took his money, produced some marketing materials, then did nothing. If you must use an agency, find one that is local and reputable, use your network to check their reputation, and work with them.

The best route to market for most inventors is licensing. You have the idea. You patent what you can patent. You build some kind of prototype. When your prototype has worked (adequately), you have 'proof of concept' and it's time to take it round big companies and secure a licensing deal whereby they do the mass production and the mass marketing. You sit back and collect the royalties (or rather collect the royalties and set out to invent more things).

The Beermat website www.beermat.biz is developing material on the precise way to do this.

Clearly, an understanding of marketing strategy is helpful in selling to these companies. Starting with the magic question 'Where's the pain?' will make your invention much, much more saleable. Understanding the target market will help you in two ways:

★ You will know which potential licensers serve those markets and are always on the lookout for new products that will really add value for people in those markets.

★ Having identified potential licensers, it will be much easier to sell to them when you show you have thought through your product from the customer viewpoint.

The more market research you can do to develop the case for your product the better.

So, having done this, why not go the whole hog and market the thing? Because it's not what most inventors are best at.

Inventors are not given the respect they should be in the UK. We seem to be stuck with an image of barmy old men emerging from smoke-filled potting sheds. TV seems determined to keep this stereotype going. Modern inventors should challenge that stereotype by taking a marketing approach to what they invent, and thinking very carefully about which route to market to follow.

Don't let dreams of million-pound enterprises or the promises of dodgy agencies send you down the wrong road. For most of you, licensing to a reputable large company is the best way forward.

Appendix B: The Product Adoption Cycle

This cycle lies at the heart of high-technology marketing – and, by extension, at the heart of any marketing effort of an innovative product. It's based on a truism – that different people have different attitudes to adopting new things – but examines these differences in a highly clear and illuminating way. The classic texts on the subject, *Diffusion of Innovations* by Everett Rogers and *Crossing the Chasm* by Geoffrey Moore, will no doubt be familiar to the directors of JEBR!

Business-to-business technology markets are often fronted by *enthusiasts,* people who love technology and buy for the hell of it. These individuals are great for testing new products on – they'll redesign it for you if you let them. But they expect everything cheap, and there aren't very many of them.

Early adopters keep a sharp eye on innovative products, not for their own sake, but in order to solve problems. Pure technical wizardry leaves them cold, but if they can see a new way of using something to solve pain, they'll take the plunge. And – here's the really good news – they'll pay good money, unlike enthusiasts.

The danger with early adopters is that they will have their

own agenda for the new technology, which can divert your development efforts away from the goal you should be aiming for, which is a product that is easy to use and which works well in a range of situations determined by the next set of users, the early majority. Instead, the early adopter may want you to work on specific features to accommodate their specific issues. There's no easy answer here: you need these people's help to start with, so just be aware of the danger of 'overcustomisation'.

In consumer markets, early adopters tend to be driven by the desire to be the first person in the street with an X. Like their business counterparts, they'll pay well for this: the first CD players set early adopter consumers back £1,200.

These two archetypes only take up about 15% of the market. Most customers belong in the next two segments.

The *early majority* are much less imaginative than the early adopters. They will pile in, in big numbers, but only once it is clear exactly what pain the new product solves, exactly how it does it, and how effectively. They will expect both greater reliability and a much lower cost. This might sound like taking a step backwards – higher standards, lower price – but this is the time when market leaders emerge and begin to sprint ahead of their competition. There will be nice, clear product definitions generally accepted by everyone; the leaders will have their manufacturing and delivery understood and will be able to drive their costs down; this new segment of the market is big (about 35%), and will place large orders. This is where fortunes are made.

The *late majority* (another 35%) wait even longer than the early majority, sitting patiently on the sidelines until a clear 'market leader' emerges, from whom they will insist on buying. (They might buy from a 'me-too' number two provider.)

For completeness, there are also *laggards*, a final 15% who never buy innovative stuff, period. The only way to sell anything new to them is to pretend it isn't new.

JEBR will be making their way round the cycle. Right now, they should have found enthusiastic techies buried deep in their large corporate potential customer-base who will be good early co-developers of the technology, getting the stuff to work. They must then move on to early adopters. These people will also co-develop, though their focus will be on *uses* of the technology. By the time they are ready to take on the early majority, JEBR must have clearly defined and reliable products, and be seen to be among the top suppliers in the world. Late majority buyers will insist on outright 'market leadership': JEBR must be number one or two in their niche.

Many hi-tech companies fail to make the move from enthusiasts and early adopters. Selling to those markets can largely be done on word of mouth, but the kind of people who make early majority purchasing decisions are very different from enthusiasts and early adopters. They are more cautious, more corporate. Worst of all, they are not particularly impressed by the recommendations of enthusiasts and early adopters, considering such people unreliable. So all the effort that has gone into getting a buzz going about the new product among the enthusiasts and early adopters will be wasted once success becomes about convincing early majority customers. You have to start your marketing all over again – and a very different kind of marketing. This is a 'chasm' that needs to be crossed.

The cycle also affects our other entrepreneurs, though less forcefully. Elspeth's therapies are not taken seriously by many people. She is effectively selling to enthusiasts and early adopters. Once therapy becomes mainstream, everyone will want it – which should sound great for Elspeth, except for the fact that big companies will enter her market at this moment. As she does not seek to build a company but just create a lifestyle, this shouldn't be a problem for her: she may have to stop selling her therapies to individuals and start doing deals with, for example, BUPA. This could actually be a real opportunity for her – the new market entrants may not know that much about complementary therapy, and she could negotiate a nice whack advising them.

Seb and Maggie are probably selling to early adopter customers, too. They will need to get ready to fend off attempts by the big brands to sell fair-trade clothing – which they should do by offering personal service and an imaginative range of clothes in their shop, but above all by showing *passion for what they do*. They will find their prices under attack, though. They will have to consider what they can do to keep value in their products and thus support their prices.

Harminder and Jat are already selling to an early majority. However, I don't see their market being threatened by big providers the way the product adoption cycle model predicts. Design will always be a personal thing. How reassuring: no theoretical model is perfect!

Appendix C: The Ten Commandments of Small Business Marketing

1. Have the marketing mindset.

2. Target. Find market segments and give them exactly what they need. For many small businesses, the internet has made this much easier.

3. Have a USP, even if it's only 10% better, nicer or easier.

4. Do all you can to establish credibility.

5. Understand the feature/benefit distinction, and how it applies to what you are offering the market.

6. It's a team game. Encourage allies and evangelists.

7. Make it easy and enjoyable for customers to buy.

8. Make some noise! Be creative about doing so, and enjoy it.

9. Always measure the effect of your marketing with numbers.

10. Your most valuable resource is the goodwill of your existing customers.

And if I were asked to name just one of these? Most of the marketing people I speak to say 'the first', and I'm totally with them. Start with the marketing mindset, and you will naturally create marketing ideas that appeal to customers. Start without it, and all the clever techniques in the world won't stop it being a long, hard and essentially puzzling slog.

Recommended Reading and Resources

Everyone has their favourite reads – apologies if something you love is not on this list (email me and tell me!).

I like the books of Jay Conrad Levinson, the originator of the term 'guerrilla marketing'. He has written a number of books, all, to be honest, largely with the same messages – read at least one of them.

I also enjoy reading marketing books by Al Ries and Jack Trout, even though they are really for people working in corporations. They exude a passion for the subject.

The Small Business Marketing Bible by David Frey is a general introduction to the topic. It's not cheap (his business model is to sell the book over the internet, which allows him to set his own price), but contains good material.

In *Marketing Judo* by John Barnes and Richard Richardson, the authors show, from their own entrepreneurial experience, how you can use the power of big brands and celebrities to leverage your brand.

Louise Third's ebook *PR on a Beermat* develops the themes outlined in Chapter 9. Download it from www.beermat.biz.

(Come and visit our site anyway – there's plenty of good stuff on there!) Talking of Beermat materials, *Sales on a Beermat* should be seen as a companion to the book you are now reading, especially if you are a marketing person keen to understand how salespeople operate.

I've already recommended *Diffusion of Innovations* by Everett Rogers and *Crossing the Chasm* by Geoffrey Moore to hi-tech entrepreneurs – and would extend that to any entrepreneur with an innovative product or business model.

Selling the Invisible by Harry Beckwith is a classic text on how to market services.

Anyone setting up a 'selling-to-customers-from-premises' business should read the Hashemis' *Anyone Can Do It*. This isn't specifically a marketing book, but it conveys well the business of marketing a new retail venture.

If you are writing ad copy, then John Caples' *Tested Advertising Methods* remains a classic.

www.subhub.com is a site with many excellent articles on online marketing, site design etc., aimed at the more ambitious site owner.

Pure internet marketers need to look on the internet to find the latest material. There are plenty of gurus out there to choose from. If you are going to get seriously into this, the training materials from Derek Gehl's Internet Marketing Centre are recommended – though watch out for the extra costs (does it really cost $50 to send two folders to the UK?) and forceful upselling. Ian Traynor is a UK-based webmaster dealing in similar material.

If you are looking for marketing advice, I can recommend the businesses of the people who have helped with this book. I choose my experts carefully!

★ Technology companies should visit www.qi3.co.uk and www.tonywilson.org.

★ www.sweetapple.co.uk is an excellent general marketing site.

★ For PR, go to www.integracommunications.co.uk.

★ Two excellent design agencies (working with both online and traditional materials) are www.mwadesign.com (based in London), and www.four-group.co.uk (based in Bristol).

★ www.wellspark.co.uk provide content for websites and media consultancy generally.

Also, please visit the sites of those entrepreneurs who have helped with this book, to see good marketing in action.

★ www.figleaves.com

★ www.zyb.com (Ed Bussey's current venture)

★ www.creativitymatters.co.uk (Stephen King)

★ www.insightassociates.co.uk (Garry Mumford)

★ www.quickformations.com (Richard Osborne).

Finally, if you have enjoyed this book, do let me know. Authors spend too much time sitting alone with computers, and like to hear from readers. If you have any simple marketing queries, do ask them — I always reply to emails. And, of course, if you want to book me to speak or do a piece of consultancy, then I'd be delighted. Contact me on chris@beermat.biz.

Index

ALSO AVAILABLE IN RANDOM HOUSE BUSINESS BOOKS

Finance on a Beermat

Stephen King, Jeff Macklin & Chris West

The Beermat team tackle finance

The Beermat Entrepreneurs are highly successful small business advisers, and in *Finance on a Beermat* they offer brilliantly straightforward and practical guidance on how to understand and take control of your company's finances. Ranging from coverage of the nuts and bolts of everyday business (how balance sheets work, what VAT returns involve) to advice on drawing up a business plan, their advice will be invaluable to anyone involved in running a company or small enterprise.

The *Beermat* guides: helping you build a great business

BUSINESS
BOOKS

Sales on a Beermat

Mike Southon & Chris West
With a foreword by Stephen Fry

Bestselling authors of *The Beermat Entrepreneur* tackle sales

The Beermat entrepreneurs are highly successful small business advisers, and in *Sales on a Beermat* they demystify the most important skill that any business can possess: selling. Ranging from coverage of the basics of organising a sales team and calling on customers to insights into the psychology of successful selling, their advice will be invaluable to anyone involved in selling, particularly those running or working for small enterprises.

The *Beermat* guides: helping you build a great business

BUSINESS
BOOKS

Order more *Beermat* guides from your local bookshop, or have them delivered direct to your door by Bookpost

Finance on a Beermat	Stephen King, Jeff Macklin & Chris West	9781847940070	£8.99
Sales on a Beermat	Mike Southon & Chris West	9781847940063	£8.99

Free post and packing
Overseas customers allow £2 per paperback

Phone: 01624 677237

Post: Random House Books
c/o Bookpost, PO Box 29, Douglas, Isle of Man IM99 1BQ

Fax: 01624 670923

email: bookshop@enterprise.net

Cheques (payable to Bookpost) and credit cards accepted

Prices and availability subject to change without notice.
Allow 28 days for delivery.
When placing your order, please state if you do not wish to receive
any additional information.

www.rbooks.co.uk

rh
BUSINESS
BOOKS